D1336632

THE FAT PIG FARM BOOK OF PRESERVES, PICKLES & SAUCES

# NOT *Just* JAM

## MATTHEW EVANS
with Michelle Crawford

# NOT *Just* JAM

THE FAT PIG FARM BOOK OF PRESERVES, PICKLES & SAUCES

## MATTHEW EVANS

with Michelle Crawford

MURDOCH BOOKS

SYDNEY · LONDON

# Contents

When you live as we do, what you eat is driven by the season; by what nature gives you. And, inevitably, you end up with a glut of one thing or another. This glut really is a gift. It allows you to store food, to preserve food, for leaner times.

This book is Fat Pig Farm's ode to the surplus of the seasons. By necessity we're glued to the stove at various times of year, harnessing the bounty of each month and squirrelling it away for other times. Overwhelmed by ripe fruit, or mountains of rhubarb, we have found ways to preserve what we grow, and what grows near us.

But this book isn't just for those who have their own orchard. It's for those passionate about flavour, who want to know what goes into their preserves. It's for the freegan, those who scour the suburbs looking for fruit trees whose bounty isn't being harvested. It's for the cook who wants their dishes to resonate with the tastes borne from their own hands. Anyone can pickle onions to use all year, or make apple syrup to drizzle over pancakes. Lunches made with homemade brown pickle are always the better for the addition. A cheese platter benefits from preserved cherries, your morning toast is lifted by your own Gentlemen's Marmalade, and a bowl of ice cream is made indulgent by the addition of gooseberry and sour cherry syrup that you've crafted in your own kitchen.

Use this book as your launching pad. You can experiment with your own flavours for preserved fruit and adjust the jams to suit your garden, your region, your palate. The piccalilli is just one variation based on what's available in the season. A pantry groaning with full jars is the sign of a life well lived, a future well catered for. And to this end, we offer the best of what's on the shelves at Fat Pig Farm.

# ❧ PRESERVING BASICS ❧

It seems, when you look at it from afar, such a crazy thing to make your own preserves. To bottle your own jam, or tomato sauce, when such things are in every supermarket, every food store in the country. But then, when you taste the intensity of a homemade Worcestershire, or feel the summer sun trapped in your strawberry conserve, you understand.

Sure, you don't have to make these things, but everybody can. They're not technically difficult, and in many ways they are on the easier end of the cooking spectrum. (If anything, jam can be harder to master than brown sauce.) What's more, a small amount of your own mustard or fruit syrup or marmalade can enhance innumerable meals.

This is the book—and these are the recipes—that show you how.

## ⇥ GENERAL RULES ⇤

Okay, so if you want to put things up for a rainy day, if you want to store and preserve and stockpile your harvest (or other people's harvests!) when the ingredients are in peak season, there are some rules. Yep, boring old rules. But by following a few simple instructions, your jam will set. Your sauce won't ferment. Your fruit won't go mouldy. There are only a handful of rules, but by following them you're far more assured of success. Ignore them you may, but it could be at your peril.

We've given you instructions on how to sterilise your bottles and jars; how to store them; how to tell if your jelly is right; and how to avoid your jam getting sugar crystals in it. Once you've mastered these, you may well come up with your own techniques, your own routines, but if you're new to the world of putting stuff in jars to eat months later, it's worth having a good read through now, and perhaps refreshing your memory before you cook each recipe, just to be sure the effort you put in today will give you a surfeit of great things to eat later.

## STERILISATION

This is the big one. In the age of refrigeration we've often forgotten how much mould and yeast thrive when left unchecked. You can preserve things through excluding oxygen (tight-fitting lids), introducing an acid (pickled foods), and by adding enough sugar or salt. But even then it's important to start with really clean implements, and to store things in sterilised jars with sterile lids. So wash your storing jars or containers really well before sterilising.

### THE HEAT METHOD

*(a dishwasher is a good place to start)*

Heat kills bugs, and bugs can cause your preserves to lose quality, or even go off. If you want to sterilise just one bottle, or a few jars, you can place them in a saucepan of cold water, on their sides, making sure they're full of water and submerged. Put their lids in there too. Bring this pot to the boil and simmer for 10 minutes. This will kill just about all the bugs you're worried about. The only downside of this method is that it is a little tricky to take hot bottles from a pot of boiling water, though there are special tongs on the market to help you. A good thing to note is that hot sauces and jams will crack a cold jar, and this method allows you to have your jars prewarmed ready to pour in a hot conserve.

Dishwashers, with a hot rinse cycle, also sterilise the jars, so that could be an easier method.

Be sure, when dealing with hot jars, not to put them onto a cold surface or they will crack. Always put them onto a wooden board. Cold jars will also crack if they have very hot things put in them, so warm the jars a little first, using warm water or similar.

### THE MICROWAVE METHOD

Don't do this to the wrong type of lid—metal ones—but jars can be sterilised effectively in the microwave because yeasts and bacteria are killed while the glass stays inert. Simply put the jars and lids in the microwave for 1 minute on High.

### THE CHEMICAL METHOD

There are commonly available sterilising chemicals, such as sodium metabisulphite, that act to kill bugs. Most are diluted in water, and you simply immerse the bottles for a few minutes. Some people prefer to avoid these chemicals; particularly those on septic systems, as the sterilising liquid can interfere with the good work the bacteria in your septic tank get up to. Home-brew shops are a great place to find sterilising chemicals that are easy to use and cheap. The baby supplies aisle of the supermarket is another place to look, though (like so many things to do with babies) the prices tend to be steeper.

## PASTEURISATION

Along with sterilisation, there's a method called pasteurisation that is used, but only on occasion. Most commonly associated with milk, this is a way of heating a product to kill the bugs that might cause a problem during storage. The time and temperature varies widely depending on what you're storing. Meat and fish, for example, have to be superheated to ensure they're safe, and it's hard to do it at home.

Things in this book, however, such as fruit syrups, vegetables or pickles, are far easier to make safe. Most things in this book don't even need a pasteurisation step, especially if they're bottled and sealed when hot. Mostly, the pasteurisation we do is to stop something fermenting, and to increase the shelf life outside of the fridge. That means you're using pantry space not fridge space.

To pasteurise something, seal it in the jar or bottle according to the recipe. Place it in a large saucepan; I like to put a tea towel (dish towel) underneath the bottles to stop them getting in direct contact with the base of the pan where the heat hits. Fill the pan with water: for some preserved fruit the water doesn't need to cover the bottles, but for most things, cover the bottles with the same temperature water as the contents to avoid glass shock and breakages. Bring the water to the boil over medium–high heat, turn down and simmer, usually for an hour or two, depending on the product. Allow the bottles to cool in the water, ideally, so you can handle them safely. Remove, dry them, label them and store in the pantry.

---

**SOME PASTEURISATION TIMES**

750 ml (26 fl oz/3 cup) bottles of an already cooked sauce: *45 minutes–1 hour*

750 ml bottles of tomato passata: *2 hours*

1 litre (35 fl oz/4 cup) bottles: *add an extra 15 minutes*

---

## STORING

The rules for storing your preserves are fairly common sense to most cooks. Heat and light are the enemy of quality most of the time, so a cool, dark place is ideal. Somewhere that has air, so it doesn't breed mould, is also handy. Think of a dry cellar as the perfect place, because it's really stable in temperature and unlikely to get above 10–12°C (50–54°F). But a pantry that is closed, that doesn't get too warm, is just about as good. Our suggested storage times are based on a decent home pantry that is relatively cool and dark compared to the rest of the house. In tropical climes, you'll want to shorten those times as need be.

## JARS AND BOTTLES

You can use any jar that seals well and can be cleaned properly. Generally a jar that has a wide opening is better, as is one that ideally holds about 300 ml (10½ fl oz), which is about the right amount of jam to have open at one time. For bottles, we tend to use big-mouthed ones for most uses, including passata and tomato sauce, though in a pinch we use beer bottles. The big downside is that if the sauce is nicely thick, it's hard to get from a beer bottle, and you can't see how much is in the bottle (or, in the case of passata, if the top has gone a little, ahem, mouldy after being left in the fridge for too long).

We reuse jars and bottles constantly, discarding any with chipped edges, and always checking the lids to ensure they're still able to seal. For our preserves we use Fowlers jars, with their reusable lids and spring clips, and sometimes Ball canning jars, which are simpler to use, though nowhere near as robust.

# ✤ JAMS ✦

Oh, jam. That simple concoction of fruit and sugar. How difficult can it be?

Well, it's beguilingly easy and deceivingly hard. You can make a passable jam, especially out of certain fruit, such as apricots, with very little practice. Even a very good jam. But to make a perfect strawberry jam, with its precocious setting point and fragile fragrance, which is readily lost during cooking? That's a bit harder to master.

Don't be afraid. The good thing is, your jam won't taste like someone else's. You'll get better every time you make it, and any decent friend will be more than ecstatic to take an experimental batch off your hands if it hasn't set.

There are, however, a few tips to help make your jam as good as it can be. Here is a list of things we think really matter.

## THE PAN

Oh, the pan. Yes, the pan. You can make jam in any saucepan. But if you want a really great jam, a specialist jam pan is pretty much essential. The reason is that you want to heat your jam quickly and evenly. You want low sides so that any superfluous moisture evaporates quickly.

Jam pans are big, wide things, with a great conductive base, such as copper (though aluminium is second best). The good ones have some weight to them to help distribute heat.

The sides flare out, making it easy to stir your jam, while at the same time these low, flared sides help liquids evaporate quicker, too.

You can use a saucepan, but make it a wide rather than tall one, and ideally one with a solid, heavy base.

Just a note about copper jam pans: it's only when you add sugar to the pan that it's considered food safe, so precooked fruit

---

### WHAT EXACTLY ARE JAMS, JELLIES, MARMALADES, PRESERVES, COMPOTES AND CONSERVES?

Okay, so the goalposts move, but this is our version, based on our Australian location and our history. A jam is a set spread that has chunks of fruit in it. A jelly is a clear-set spread, where the fruit has been sifted out. A marmalade is usually made with citrus, so it's a citrus jam, really. Though we love the term marmalade. Reminds us of Paddington Bear and good things to spread on toast. A conserve is a jam, really. A compote can be a very, very chunky jam. And a preserve, for our purposes, is a preserved whole or cut fruit, in a bottle or jar, that has little or no sugar added (though in other places a preserve can be a jam, too).

---

(such as for marmalade) is best transferred to the jam pan only when the sugar is added.

## OTHER EQUIPMENT

Apart from the pan, there are a few other bits and pieces that help to make a good jam. One is the spatula. My friend Michelle, who helped compile recipes for this book, taught me that the best stirring implement is a silicone-ended spatula. It's a little bit flexible and it's heatproof. The end doesn't scratch your pan, but it does let you feel exactly how the jam is going. Is it catching? Is it thickening? How much is it boiling, underneath? It's amazing what you can feel through a good spatula.

Another useful tool is a stainless steel funnel with a wide mouth. These funnels allow you to fill jars more easily without getting jam or jelly all over the sides of the jars.

You may want a jelly bag, if you're getting into jelly making in more than just a tiny way. But in the interim you can use muslin (cheesecloth) or even clean porous kitchen cleaning cloths or similar cloths.

And there are special tongs for getting hot jars out of boiling water, which can be handy if you're boiling your jars to sterilise them.

## THE FRUIT

When you're making a jam, the whole point is to preserve as much of the charm, the aroma, the flavour of the fruit as possible. Sure, you may want to sift out some of the seeds in your raspberry jam, or cut your strawberries smaller, but regardless of all that, bad quality fruit ain't gonna make for great jam. Ripe fruit, by definition, has the best flavour. That said, jam also tastes better with some acid, which you tend to get in slightly under-ripe fruit. This also helps the set, so the perfect jam has some ripe and some under-ripe fruit. I reckon about a maximum of a quarter of the total can be a little under-ripe. If you only have extremely ripe fruit, you may want to consider adding jam sugar to help the set.

Where we live, because we're based among the growers, we can tell that fruit harvested after rain has more moisture. So, ideally, we don't use fruit harvested at that time, as this extra liquid makes for longer cooking times to get a nice set. Don't use this as an excuse not to make any jam, however, as it's still better to use local fruit, in season, than to not make jam at all.

## THE SUGAR

Okay, so it's just sugar, right? Well, it is, and it isn't. For many uses normal sugar is just fine with jams and preserving. But for making jam, the way the sugar dissolves, and how long it takes, is relevant to the end product.

Generally, you want the sugar dissolved fast (but not over too-high heat, as it might crystallise out later). And while the sugar dissolves, the fruit is cooking, which could, in the case of some more fragile fruit, lend itself to overcooking.

There are two ways to dissolve the sugar quicker and avoid that problem. One is by warming the sugar so it's already closer to the temperature you'll want it to be. Another is to macerate the fruit in sugar (see below). In all cases, it's best to start the jam on a moderate rather than a huge heat, stirring it constantly until the sugar has dissolved, then you can increase the heat in the jam pan so it gets to a rollicking boil, which in turn will get to the set as quickly as possible.

For some jams, and if you're a beginner in particular, there's a specialist sugar you may want to try called 'jam sugar' that has pectin mixed in and helps with the set. You can also use caster (superfine) sugar as it dissolves more quickly, too.

### MACERATING

Macerating, where you toss the fruit in the sugar and leave it for a time, works in two ways. It helps to draw moisture out of the fruit, altering the texture, and it helps to dissolve the sugar. Many top jam makers will macerate the fruit in the sugar for a few hours or overnight to ensure a better texture. You can be more sure of a soft, gently set jam using maceration so it's a pretty great idea to have in your armoury. Sometimes I do it, sometimes not.

## STIRRING

A good jam is stirred pretty much the whole time while the sugar dissolves, and then regularly after that. Stirring does a few things. It obviously stops the jam from catching on the bottom of the pan. By catching, I mean the first step as the fruit and sugars start to scorch. You can feel it under the spoon. But if you use a silicone spatula or similar, as you run it over the bottom of the pan, you can tell how the jam is cooking. You

can actually feel the effect of the heat, and how thick the jam is, while some stirring evens up the cooking of the jam as you distribute the heat throughout the fruit. Which isn't a bad thing. Just don't stir too much or you'll cool the jam and increase the cooking time.

## COOKING TIMES

Each fruit has a different cooking time. Generally, soft fruit is more delicate than firmer fruit. So a marmalade can be cooked longer than a raspberry jam. Usually, you want a jam cooked in under 15 minutes if you can, unless stated otherwise. That said, an apricot jam or similar can be cooked a little longer with virtually no adverse effect.

# ⇥‖ SETTING AND SETTING AGENTS ‖⇤

A jam and jelly are tested for what's called a 'set' or 'the set'. That's the moment when the sugar, fruit, water and a thing called pectin are in harmony so the jam isn't going to be a liquid any more once cooled. The easiest way to test a set is to put a saucer in the freezer, remove the jam from the heat so it doesn't overcook, and dribble a little jam onto the cold saucer. Leave it for 30 seconds and if your finger running across the drop of jam causes it to wrinkle, then the setting point has been reached. Some people swear by using a thermometer to check the set. Jam will set at 105°C (220°F), though I prefer the manual method as it keeps you watching the colour of the jam, which is a great indicator of quality. This process works well for jellies, too. Look for the wrinkle after the jelly has been dribbled onto a chilled saucer and you run your fingernail across it.

To get a perfect set is the jam maker's art; not too solid or it's rubbery and difficult to spread. Not too runny, or it's a sauce. I like my jams and jellies softer rather than firmer, myself. Jam setting is affected by a confluence of things. There's the sugar, which, simply added to water in sufficient quantity, will cause the water to become thicker once cooled. There's the acidity in the fruit, which is important because higher-acid fruits lend themselves to a better set. (You'll see we quite often add acid, in the form of fresh lemon juice, to the jams in this book to help them set.) The fruit pulp itself can make for a thicker jam, depending on the type of fruit and how it's distributed. And there's this thing called pectin, which is the magic agent in fruit that helps a jam or jelly set. The good news is that you can add pectin and adjust the acid for low-pectin fruits to help them set. Pectin is available at most supermarkets, often in the form of a ready-to-use sugar, called 'jam sugar'.

Jam making is chemistry, really. And like a cake recipe that can fail if you change the proportions, so can a jam recipe. Think the recipe looks too high in sugar and so you cut it down a bit? You'll not only make the resulting jam less sweet, but likely make it runnier or have to cook it longer. Sugar helps pectin do its job, so using less is likely to cause changes you weren't expecting. Sugar is also a preservative, so using less can mean your jam goes mouldy more easily.

## WHAT TO DO WITH A POORLY SET JAM

Poorly set jam, be it too hard or too soft, is a bit of a bummer, but hardly the end of the world. If it's a bit firm, you can loosen it up in a saucepan over low heat with a little extra water, and use it in recipes (if you do this and re-jar it, it tends to crystallise, but it's worth a shot if you want).

If it's a bit too runny, simply use it as a sauce, purée it for milkshake flavouring, or stir it through ice cream and refreeze to make a rippled dessert. A runny jam, however, is more likely to go mouldy sooner, so keep an eye on it.

## DON'T BE TEMPTED TO DOUBLE RECIPES

Just don't. Jam cooking combines a number of really important steps. Doubling or tripling recipes is—excuse the cliché—a recipe for disaster. You'll increase the time it takes to get the jam to a simmer, which in turn will lower the quality of the end product. It'll take longer to get to the set, again leading to poorer flavour and aroma. In other words, you're better off to do two batches than double one batch. If we ever want to make a larger amount, we may use two pans instead of one, but we never double the amount in the pan.

# ⇻ PRESERVING FRUIT ⇺

## JARS & PRESERVING EQUIPMENT

We tend to use big old preserving jars that we buy locally, that have a replaceable rubber seal, and a reusable lid and spring. Made by Fowlers, these are the standard preserving jar, with a neck virtually as wide as the jar, great thick glass that can withstand hard knocks and heat, and they come in good, large sizes. Other brands are available, but large jars are essential. To sterilise your jars, see page 10.

In terms of equipment, I like to use my old copper preserving pan, which is very tall and has a tight-fitting lid. The water only comes part way up the jars before a hole in the side of the pan spills it out. There's a place for a thermometer to check the temperature, and the jars can easily be picked up using some purpose-built jar tongs that you can buy at decent hardware stores and shops.

## THE RULES

Generally, the rules are pretty straightforward when preserving fruit. Try to get plenty of fruit in each jar and stack it neatly, as the jar becomes a little advertisement of what's inside and they look grand on a shelf.

Use only a small amount of sugar, or none at all, if that's what you want.

Try to get as many bubbles out from underneath the fruit after you add the water, to ensure there's enough to cover the fruit so it preserves properly.

Only fill the jars with liquid to a maximum of 1 cm (⅜ inch) from the top, which allows for expansion as the jars are simmered to pasteurise the contents. Check jars have sealed after pasteurising, and any that haven't should be put into the fridge and consumed first.

## WHAT—HOW—WHY?

Preserving is a great way to use up surplus fruit. Most fruits can be preserved in jars, as can tomatoes. Simply put as much clean fruit as you can in a jar, fill it with water, seal it and simmer it. That's it. After it's simmered (pasteurised) it stores in the pantry.

Don't, however, try to preserve bruised or damaged fruit. This is likely to ferment or go off, which isn't a great outcome. Use ripe or very-nearly-ripe fruit, and do a big batch at one time. The recipes we've given are a base. Unlike jam, you'll be doing yourself a favour if you can fill at least one big pot with jars at a time.

# ⇥| PICKLES |⇤

## WHAT TO PICKLE

You can pickle most things, though some
are better than others. We've tried pickling
nasturtium seeds and mushrooms, with success.
You can pickle zucchini (courgettes), broccoli,
carrots: anything really, but we find their uses
more limited than the recipes in this book.

## VINEGAR

Arguably the most important ingredient in your
pickle is the vinegar. And there's such a variety
of vinegars out there, you can easily mix it up
as you feel like.

However, a cheap, white vinegar distilled from
sugar cane is often the worst. It's aggressive
on the palate, adds no charm of its own and
can rob even the best ingredients of their joy.

We often use apple cider vinegar. And buy
(or use our own) wine vinegars, both white
and red, on occasion. But beware, because
sometimes a very flavoursome vinegar, such
as the cider vinegar our neighbour makes,
has too much flavour for some pickles. In that
case, a more mainstream wine vinegar is better
suited. What's good in a salad dressing isn't
always what's good in the jar. Suitable vinegars,
it's good to know, can be found at most decent
supermarkets these days.

One thing you can be sure of: bad-tasting
vinegar will lead to a bad-tasting pickle, so don't
be too tight when deciding what vinegar to use.

# ⇥| SAUCES |⇤

## BOTTLES

We tend to go for reusable glass, as it's inert and
seems to make sense environmentally. See the
jam section (page 10) for more information on
sterilising the bottles.

## MATURATION

Most sauces benefit from some maturation.
Even tomato sauce is better with a little time in
the bottle. The best we've made was matured for
over two years prior to using; it'd turned a bit
darker, the flavours melded better and it was,
if anything, more complex in nature.

For each recipe I've suggested a maturation
time. This is because some sauces are simply
not good for a while. But if you can resist the
temptation, things like the Worcestershire,
or the mushroom ketchup, even the Aussie
barbecue sauce, really do benefit from a year
in the bottle, which gives you the excuse to
make an even bigger batch this year.

# CHAPTER ONE:

Jams + Conserves

J am. Or call it conserve if you like. The name rolls off the tongue, as easily as a good jam, smothered on hot buttered toast, rolls onto the tongue. A good jam is a sign of a considered life. If you don't have a nice jam in the cupboard, you're not really eating as well as you could. After all, with such great jam makers in so many country towns, and even some pretty good jams available at supermarkets, there's really no excuse for mediocrity.

And yet, to make jam is the simplest and hardest of things. It's just sugar and fruit, really. But to make it perfectly, well, that's a bit of an art (see the pages at the front of the book for more tips). Yet, making jam is a pure expression of the seasons. You are harnessing the summer's sun, or the fragrance of autumn fruit. You're capturing the essence of hedgerows, or the bounty of the trees.

Jam is more than just a spread. It's a window into the way you live, and how much dignity you have about what you put in your mouth.

Or maybe it's just something sweet to give the kids after school, or the missus before she races off to work. Whichever way, good jam is important enough to get its own chapter.

# STRAWBERRY JAM:
## ⇥| THE RULES |⇤

Okay, so we all love strawberry jam. But it's actually a tricky jam to master. Don't worry, however, if you fail. As long as it's not overcooked, it'll still taste fantastic even if it's runny. We even based our pancake Sundays on the fact I'd bottled a lot of jam that had the consistency of sauce.

## TIMING

Strawberries are one of the more sensitive fruits. They overcook quickly, and the ideal cooking time is 8 minutes. Yep, seriously, 8 minutes. Overcooking can leave the jam lacklustre in colour and flavour. You can cook it longer, but the risk is that you'll lose quality. For the Pimm's version (see page 32), we don't use jam sugar, but cook it for longer.

## SETTING

This is where cooking times are a problem. It's unlikely your jam will set in the 8 minutes it takes to cook a good jam. Hence, many people suggest the addition of a little pectin (generally the most common way is by using so-called 'jam sugar' with added pectin: see page 17), which is probably the easiest method. If forced to decide on cooking for longer or less time, I prefer a loose-set jam than a hard set, because I like to preserve the flavour of the fruit. That could mean some mould on the jam, or that it simply is too runny for toast. In that case, it's ideal on ice cream or pancakes instead!

# TEXTBOOK STRAWBERRY JAM

**MAKES 1.8 KG (4 LB)**

1 kg (2 lb 4 oz) strawberries, some slightly unripe fruit in the mix makes it perfect

900 g (2 lb) jam sugar, warmed (see page 17)

juice of 2 lemons, strained

*Wash and sterilise seven 300 ml (10½ fl oz) jars (see page 10).*

Hull the strawberries and cut them in half. Put them in a jam pan or similar over medium heat, add the sugar and stir well as the sugar melts. When the sugar has melted, add the lemon juice and turn up the heat to fairly high. Cook the jam for 8 minutes. Turn off and test for the set (see page 18). Ideally, the jam is at setting point and can be transferred to sterile jars. If not, return the jam pan to high heat and cook only for another 2 minutes, then remove from the heat and test the set again.

If it still hasn't reached a set (it should've, if you've used jam sugar), then you've a choice. Bottle it now and use the resulting bright red, richly fragrant syrup for things other than toast. Or continue cooking and lose some of the fresh strawberry flavour and colour. The choice, as with all cooking, is yours.

Store in the pantry, or the fridge once opened.

# SUMMER SUN STRAWBERRY JAM

MAKES ABOUT 1.5 KG (3 LB 5 OZ)

1.2 kg (2 lb 12 oz) strawberries, hulled and halved to make 1 kg (2 lb 4 oz) hulled fruit

450 g (1 lb) sugar

juice of 1 lemon, strained

Based on an old American recipe I stumbled upon that cooks the jam in the sun. The hardest part is keeping the ants away. You want a blistering hot sunny day to cook this jam, otherwise you can cheat and cook it in a slow oven for a few hours. This jam retains the lovely fresh character of the fruit, and you're not at risk of overcooking it like a standard jam. It's also quite low in sugar, so must be kept in the fridge.

*Wash and sterilise five 300 ml (10½ fl oz) jars (see page 10).*

Toss all of the ingredients into a jam pan over medium–high heat and bring the mixture to the boil, stirring often. Once it boils, immediately remove the pan from the heat. Scrape the strawberries and all the juices into a nonreactive baking dish (glass works best) and cover well with plastic wrap. Pierce the plastic with a fine skewer, and leave in the hot sun for between 8 and 24 hours in total. A muslin (cheesecloth) cover works well too, if you're confident you can keep the bugs away. Take off the plastic wrap and give it a stir every 2 or 3 hours. Bring it inside overnight, if it's not ready on the first day, and store it in the pantry. Put it out again the next day.

When it's done, a droplet will feel sticky when pinched between your thumb and forefinger, or if you run a spoon through the dish it will leave a trace for 2 or 3 seconds.

Alternatively, you can cook it in a slow oven at 120°C (250°F) for an hour or two until the jam is a syrupy consistency.

Store in jars in the fridge; they will keep for at least 4 months.

# STRAWBERRY
# & PIMM'S JAM

MAKES ABOUT 1.8 KG (4 LB)

So, you thought you had your favourite strawberry jam recipe already, did you? Well, add a little Pimm's and see just where your favourite stands now.

*Wash and sterilise six 300 ml (10½ fl oz) jars (see page 10).*

Wash and hull the strawberries. Cut any large ones in half. Preheat the oven to 100°C (210°F).

Put the strawberries in a jam pan with the sugar and lemon juice. Stir over medium heat; the strawberries will begin to release their juices and this will get easier. When the sugar has dissolved and there is lots of juice, increase the heat to high and bring to a rapid boil, then reduce the heat to medium and continue to simmer for 20–30 minutes. Remove from the heat and check the set (see page 18). Stand in the pan for a few minutes and allow the scum to settle. Remove the scum gently with a metal spoon.

Stir through the Pimm's and immediately pour into warm jars and seal, then put the jars into the oven for 15 minutes to further sterilise. Allow to cool, then store in the pantry, or the fridge when opened.

1.1 kg (2 lb 7 oz) strawberries, about 1 kg (2 lb 4 oz) when hulled

850 g (1 lb 14 oz) sugar

80 ml (2½ fl oz/⅓ cup) lemon juice, strained

30 ml (1 fl oz) Pimm's fruit cup liqueur

# BLACKCURRANT JAM

**MAKES 1.8 KG (4 LB)**

1 kg (2 lb 4 oz) blackcurrants,
 weighed before stripping fruit
 from the stalks
750 g (1 lb 10 oz) sugar

This is a thick, rich, decadent jam that packs a punch. It's dense with the glorious flavour of blackcurrants, which spread thickly on toast. A little goes a long way, so a spoonful in icing can really transform a cake. There's a trick with blackcurrants though; cook them with water, before adding sugar, or they'll end up firm skinned and not all that nice.

*Wash and sterilise six 300 ml (10½ fl oz) jars (see page 10).*

Strip the blackcurrants from the stalks and put them in a jam pan with 200 ml (7 fl oz) of water. Bring to the boil over high heat, then reduce the heat and simmer for 10 minutes or until the fruit is soft. Better too soft than not soft enough, or the skins will be like buttons in the finished jam.

Add the sugar, increase the heat and stir while bringing it back to the boil. Reduce the heat to maintain a lively simmer and cook for about 30 minutes, stirring often, until the jam sets nicely when tested on a plate (see page 18). You'll need to keep an eye on this jam, as it is prone to catching.

Pour into warmed jars, seal and store in the pantry. Once opened, store in the fridge.

# PEAR &
# CARDAMOM JAM

**MAKES ABOUT 2 KG (4 LB 8 OZ)**

Jam isn't just about summer fruit. Here, autumn pears are spiced up with cardamom to make a warming, pulpy concoction just perfect for spreading on sourdough toast.

*Wash and sterilise seven 300 ml (10½ fl oz) jars (see page 10).*

Mix all of the ingredients together in a jam pan and put over medium heat. Cook, stirring constantly, until the sugar has dissolved. Turn up the heat and continue cooking at a lively simmer for about 30 minutes, stirring often.

Remove from the heat and check the set (see page 18). Continue cooking if necessary until setting point is reached. Remove the cardamom sachet and squeeze the cardamom flavour back into the jam. Stir, then ladle into warmed jars and store in the pantry until opened, then store in the fridge.

1 kg (2 lb 4 oz) peeled, cored and chopped pears, from about 1.5 kg (3 lb 5 oz) whole pears
zest and strained juice of 2 lemons
800 g (1 lb 12 oz/3⅔ cups) sugar
10 cardamom pods, bashed and tied up in a piece of muslin (cheesecloth) or secured in a tea ball

# HIGH DUMPSIE DEARIE

**MAKES ABOUT 2 KG (4 LB 8 OZ)**

500 g (1 lb 2 oz) pears

500 g (1 lb 2 oz) apples

500 g (1 lb 2 oz) plums

zest and strained juice of 1 lemon

1 thumb-size knob of fresh ginger, bashed

1.2 kg (2 lb 10 oz/5 cups) sugar

Although worth making for the whimsical name alone, this traditional recipe from Worcestershire is perfect for using the autumn windfall fruits. We often forage for plums on the roadside and the apples come from our orchard. They say 'plant pears for your heirs', so our trees are yet to provide enough for all our uses. But they should for my son's.

*Wash and sterilise seven 300 ml (10½ fl oz) jars (see page 10).*

Peel and core the pears and apples. Peel and stone the plums and cut all of the fruit into large chunks. Put them in a jam pan with the zest and juice of the lemon and the ginger. Add enough cold water to just cover the fruit. Bring to the boil over high heat, then reduce the heat to medium and cook for about 30 minutes until the fruit is soft.

Fish out the ginger (or leave it in if you like it spicy) and add the sugar. Stir until the sugar has dissolved then increase the heat to high. Boil rapidly for about 15 minutes, remove from the heat and check the set (see page 18).

Pour into sterilised jars and seal. Store in the pantry until opened, then store in the fridge.

# DRIED APRICOT JAM

**MAKES ABOUT 2.5 KG (5 LB 8 OZ)**

With a heightened intensity not found in fresh fruit, dried apricots make a wicked jam you can knock up in any season.

*Wash and sterilise about nine 300 ml (10½ fl oz) jars (see page 10).*

Put the apricots in a bowl with 1.5 litres (52 fl oz/6 cups) of water and soak overnight.

Put the apricots and soaking water in a large heavy-based saucepan with the cinnamon sticks. Bring to the boil over medium heat. Reduce the heat to low and simmer gently for 15 minutes or until the apricots are nice and soft, stirring occasionally.

Transfer the mixture to a jam pan, if you have one, over medium heat. Add the sugar and lemon juice. Stir frequently until the mixture comes to the boil. Reduce the heat to low so that the jam simmers gently for about 40 minutes, still stirring occasionally.

Remove from the heat and check the set (see page 18). Pour into warmed sterilised jars and seal. Store in a cool, dark place (or in the fridge, once opened) until ready to gobble down on croissants or something equally buttery.

500 g (1 lb 2 oz) dried apricots (Australian halved apricots are a great option)

2 cinnamon sticks

1 kg (2 lb 4 oz) sugar

2½ tablespoons strained lemon juice

# BLACKBERRY JAM

MAKES 1.5 KG (3 LB 5 OZ) OR A BIT OVER

A good blackberry jam is a princely thing, for a pauper's price. We gather wild blackberries from roadsides and fencelines, and there are often too many to eat fresh or bake into pies. A few pots of jam, however, and you're set for the year. Blackberries can be a bit low in pectin, and you may like to use a special jam sugar or add pectin. I prefer to give it a go without, and use any runny jam in the place of a syrup. Add a couple of mint leaves, or a little grated nutmeg, to the jam to jazz it up a bit. I actually don't mind a fresh bay leaf in mine.

1 kg (2 lb 4 oz) blackberries

900 g (2 lb) sugar

juice of 2 lemons, strained

*Wash and sterilise six 300 ml (10½ fl oz) jars (see page 10).*

Pick over the blackberries for twigs, then combine them in a bowl or saucepan with the sugar and macerate overnight, or for at least 6 hours, pressing them down a bit with a potato masher to crush lightly.

Heat the blackberry and sugar mix with the lemon juice in a jam pan or similar over medium heat, stirring pretty much constantly while the sugar dissolves completely. Turn up the heat to medium–high and cook the jam for 5 minutes. Remove from the heat and push about a third of the jam through a sieve to extract some of the seeds. It's not essential, but it's not a bad thing to do.

Return the jam to the pan over high heat, and cook for about another 5 minutes after it comes to the boil, stirring occasionally, then check the set (see page 18). It should be just about ready, though you can give it a couple more minutes if need be.

Transfer to the lightly warmed jars, cap immediately, and store in the pantry. Once opened, store in the fridge.

# APPLE MARMALADE

**MAKES ABOUT 2 KG (4 LB 8 OZ)**

750 g (1 lb 10 oz) lemons,
  scrubbed lightly

1 kg (2 lb 4 oz) apples

1 kg (2 lb 4 oz) sugar

This is a winning combination of apple and lemon, where thin strips of lemon peel are suspended in an apple flavoured jelly. It's rather good on crumpets.

*Wash and sterilise seven 300 ml (10½ fl oz) jars (see page 10).*

Juice the lemons then thinly slice the skins, reserving the membranes and seeds from the centre. Tie up the seeds and membrane in a muslin (cheesecloth) bag.

Meanwhile, prepare the apple juice: chop the apples roughly, there is no need to peel or core them but remove any bruised bits. Put the apple in a large saucepan, cover with water, add the lemon juice and muslin bag. Bring to the boil over high heat, then reduce the heat to a simmer. Cook the fruit for about 1 hour until it is very soft. Pour through a muslin-lined colander suspended over a bowl and allow to drain overnight.

Meanwhile, put the sliced lemon peel in a small saucepan, cover with water and bring to the boil. Reduce the heat to low, and just simmer until the peel is soft. This can take 30 minutes or so. Remove from the heat, allow to cool slightly, then cover and let sit overnight.

Strain the peel, discarding the liquid. Combine the peel and apple juice in a jam pan. Add the sugar and stir over medium heat until the sugar has dissolved. Crank up the heat to high and boil for about 15 minutes, stirring often, until the setting point is reached (see page 18).

Pour into warmed jars and seal. Store in the pantry until opened, then store in the fridge.

# AMBER MARMALADE

**MAKES ABOUT 2.5 KG (5 LB 8 OZ)**

Oh yes, marmalade. A three-fruit version. That perfect blend of bitterness, tartness and sweetness. Strips of peel with just the right amount of chew. A gloriously set jelly with a smoky hue. Smothered on thickly buttered toast and eaten with a steaming mug of tea? Oh yes, marmalade. I think I want some right now.

*Wash and sterilise nine 300 ml (10½ fl oz) jars (see page 10).*

Cut the fruit into quarters, and then cut across each quarter to make thin slices. Thinner is generally better with marmalade, though I do like a few larger strips on occasion. Put the slices in a large stainless steel saucepan and just cover with water. Bring to the boil over high heat, then reduce to a lively simmer for about 45 minutes until the peel is tender. Remove from the heat, cover the pan and allow to stand overnight.

The next day, pour the fruit and liquid into a jam pan over medium heat. Add the sugar and stir until dissolved. Increase the heat to high and boil the marmalade for about 30 minutes. Remove from the heat then check the set (see page 18). Pour into warmed jars and seal. It should keep well for up to 2 years in a cool, dark spot. Refrigerate once opened.

3 oranges, scrubbed gently

2 grapefruit, scrubbed gently

4 lemons, scrubbed gently

2.25 kg (5 lb/10¼ cups) sugar

# QUINCE & MEYER LEMON MARMALADE

**MAKES ABOUT 1.5 KG (3 LB 5 OZ)**

The Greeks make a fantastic quince marmalade, probably because they grow a lot of quince and have perfected many ways with the fruit. This is our version, using a little lemon peel and cardamom in the mix. Be sure to use the first cooking liquid to make a jelly or thick paste, as it's very fragrant, too.

*Wash and sterilise five 300 ml (10½ fl oz) jars (see page 10). Preheat the oven to 150°C (300°F).*

Put the quinces in a baking dish with 1 litre (35 fl oz/4 cups) of water and 2 tablespoons of the sugar. Cover with baking paper and seal well with foil, then bake for 3 hours. When done, scoop the quince carefully out of the cooking liquid, trying to keep them whole. Reserve the cooking liquid for making quince jelly (see note). Allow the quinces to cool.

While the quinces cook, juice the lemons and reserve the juice. Put the peel in a small saucepan with enough water to cover and simmer for about 1 hour until very soft. Drain and discard the water. Cut the peel into very thin strips, discarding the internal membranes.

When the quinces have cooled, remove the cores. It can be helpful to push the pulp through a sieve if it has some hard bits in it, which quinces sometimes do.

Weigh the pulp and put it with an equal weight of sugar into a jam pan with the lemon peel, cardamom and 500 ml (17 fl oz/2 cups) of water. Add the lemon juice and heat the pan over medium heat. Stir until the sugar dissolves, then turn up the heat and bring to the boil. Simmer, stirring regularly, for about 10 minutes until a set is reached (see page 18). Transfer to warmed jars, seal immediately and store in the pantry. Once opened, store in the fridge.

| |
|---|
| 1 kg (2 lb 4 oz) quince, ideally a bit under-ripe |
| about 800 g (1 lb 12 oz) sugar |
| 2 meyer lemons, scrubbed |
| ¼ teaspoon cardamom seeds |

### ·❃· QUINCE JELLY ·❃·

*You can use the cooking liquid to make a jelly, by measuring it, adding an equal amount of sugar and a squeeze of lemon juice, then cooking until it reaches a set (see page 18), which will take about an hour or so, then transfer to sterilised jars.*

# CHILLI JAM

**MAKES ABOUT 500 G (1 LB 2 OZ)**

500 ml (17 fl oz/2 cups) vegetable oil, for deep-frying

135 g (4¾ oz/1 cup) red shallots, sliced lengthways

about 100 g (3½ oz) garlic cloves, thinly sliced

3 tablespoons dried prawns (shrimp), rinsed and drained

10 dried long red chillies, seeds removed

3 slices well-scrubbed galangal (use ginger in a pinch)

a nice pinch of shrimp paste, roasted

3 tablespoons finely grated palm sugar (jaggery)

2 tablespoons thick tamarind water (see below)

1–2 tablespoons fish sauce

### ❧ TAMARIND WATER ❧

*You can buy tamarind water, but if you have the pulp, it's easy to make it yourself. It's just the pulp of preserved tamarind that is soaked in a tiny amount of boiling water, just enough to loosen it. When it's cool enough, press through a sieve, discard the seeds and keep the thickish brown liquid.*

This is a Thai-style chilli jam, which is perfect for stir-frying mussels, or adding to prawns (shrimp), or rubbing over chickens before roasting, or adding to a papaya salad. It's rich with dried prawns, and is best finished with a little fresh lime juice when you go to use it. I particularly like it with eggs, such as a crab-meat omelette or even fried eggs on rice. And if your chooks aren't laying, it's just great with a bowl of freshly steamed jasmine rice.

*Wash and sterilise two 300 ml (10½ fl oz) jars (see page 10).*

Heat the oil in a wok or small saucepan over medium to high heat. Deep-fry, separately, the red shallots, garlic, prawns and chillies. The shallots should be golden, the garlic paler than the shallots, and the prawns and chillies brown but not darkened too much. Deep-fry the galangal until it starts to brown. Drain and reserve the oil.

In a food processor, blend all of the ingredients except the palm sugar, tamarind water and fish sauce. Add enough of the reserved oil to make a paste: probably about half the oil by the end. Put this paste in a medium saucepan over medium heat, bring to a simmer then reduce the heat to low. Add the palm sugar, tamarind and fish sauce to taste and cook until it forms a nice jam consistency: this will take about 15 minutes, give or take a few. It'll thicken as it cools.

Once cool, transfer to sterilised jars and use straightaway or keep it in the fridge for up to 3 months.

# TOMATO JAM WITH A SOUTH–EAST ASIAN INFLUENCE

**MAKES ABOUT 500 G (1 LB 2 OZ)**

This is the simplified version of a lively tomato jam made with a Thai-style chilli jam base. It's wonderful on eggs, in a stir-fry, on fish or tossed with mussels and the like. The palm sugar is essential for the subtle complexity, while dried prawns (shrimp) give it another layer of flavour. Asian grocery stores will stock all the unusual ingredients.

*Wash and sterilise two or three 300 ml (10½ fl oz) jars (see page 10).*

Simmer the tomatoes in a saucepan over low heat, stirring regularly until reduced to about half the volume.

Put the oil, garlic, fried shallots, dried prawns and chilli in a small food processor and process until well broken up. Add the tomatoes and process to purée. Return to the pan and add the palm sugar, fish sauce and tamarind water, stirring until the sugar has dissolved.

The jam should be sweet, sour and slightly salty. Tomatoes vary so much in their flavour and sweetness, so let your taste be the guide and adjust the flavouring as required.

Store it in the fridge, for up to a month.

400 g (14 oz) tomatoes, chopped

1 tablespoon peanut or vegetable oil

3 garlic cloves, crushed

50 g (1¾ oz) fried shallots (crispy fried red shallots)

2 tablespoons dried prawns (shrimp), rinsed and drained

1 dried red chilli, seeds removed, soaked for 15 minutes and chopped

40 g (1½ oz) palm sugar (jaggery), coarsely chopped

2 tablespoons fish sauce

1 tablespoon tamarind water (substitute lime juice if desired) (see page 45)

# GREEN TOMATO JAM

**MAKES ABOUT 1.8 KG (4 LB)**

1 kg (2 lb 4 oz) green tomatoes

1 lemon, quartered and
thinly sliced

800 g (1 lb 12 oz/3⅔ cups) sugar

½ teaspoon salt

1 vanilla bean

This is a jam, not a pickle, so don't be tempted to use it in places where you don't want a lot of sugar. It's one of the ways we tend to use up the inevitable crop of tomatoes that is racing to ripen before the cold weather takes hold. The fruit that loses the race can easily end up here.

*Wash and sterilise six 300 ml (10½ fl oz) jars (see page 10).*

Quarter each tomato and cut each quarter crossways into thin slices. Put the tomatoes, lemon slices, sugar and salt in a large bowl. Toss this so the tomatoes are covered in sticky, lemony sugar, then cover with plastic wrap and allow to stand overnight.

The next day, transfer the mixture to a jam pan. With a small paring knife, slice the vanilla bean open lengthways. Scrape the seeds out and toss them into the pan along with the bean.

Set the pan over medium heat and bring the mixture to a boil, stirring to combine the ingredients and dissolve the sugar, then reduce to a lively simmer and cook for about 45 minutes, stirring often. You want to cook it until it's glossy and thick enough to spread. Remove the vanilla bean and pour into warmed jars and seal. Store in a cool dry place.

**NOTE:** *You could replace the vanilla with a tablespoon of grated fresh ginger if you like. (I'm not a great fan of ginger in jam—just one of my personal quirks—but ginger does add an intriguing kick if you like the flavour.)*

# LATE SUMMER PEACH JAM WITH AMARETTO

**MAKES ABOUT 3 KG (6 LB 12 OZ)**

A good peach jam is a mighty fine thing. I'd never heard of such a thing when I was a lad. This is a lovely combination of the grown-up bitterness of amaretto with the heady fragrance of good peaches.

*Wash and sterilise ten 300 ml (10½ fl oz) jars (see page 10).*

Cut the peaches in half, then quarters, remove the stones, then slice each quarter into thin wedges. Reserve the stones in a container in the fridge.

Put the peaches in a large glass or ceramic bowl, then add the sugar and lemon juice and stir well. Lay some plastic wrap on the surface to stop the peaches discolouring, then cover the entire bowl in more plastic wrap and refrigerate overnight. (Actually, you can leave it for up to 2 days if you like.)

The next day, get the stones and crack them open, removing the little kernels inside. Yes, it is a bit of a pain, but think of how you'll end up with ten—yes, TEN—jars of jam! Tie the kernels in a muslin (cheesecloth) bag.

Pour the peach mixture into a large jam pan, making sure to scrape in all the sugar and juices clinging to the bowl. Add the bag of kernels and put the pan over medium heat, stirring until the sugar dissolves. Bring to the boil over high heat, stirring often. Reduce the heat slightly to maintain a healthy gallop and cook until the jam starts to thicken, anywhere from 25 to 40 minutes. Remove from the heat and check the set (see page 18). If it's ready, remove the bag of kernels carefully with a pair of tongs, then add the amaretto to taste and stir through.

Pour into warmed jars and seal. Best opened in the dead of winter. Store in the pantry until opened, then in the fridge.

2 kg (4 lb 8 oz) late summer yellow peaches, a combination of ripe peaches and some that are a little green to get a higher pectin level

1 kg (2 lb 4 oz) sugar

120 ml (4 fl oz) lemon juice, strained (you will need about 6 lemons)

2–3 tablespoons amaretto

# GREENGAGE JAM

**MAKES ABOUT 2 KG (4 LB 8 OZ)**

In this recipe, the glorious greengage—my favourite plum—is allowed to shine all on its own. It's cooked with the stones in, as the plums are a bit of a drag to pit, and the cooked jam is put through a mouli or sieve to remove them prior to bottling. You don't have to do that, but if you don't, you will want to warn anybody who eats the jam that they will have plenty of plum stones to contend with on their toast. As possibly the finest of plums, greengages are a rare treat and it's even better if you know someone with a tree in their backyard. I like to use minimal sugar and keep this jam in the fridge, a small price to pay to preserve the soft delicate flavour of the aromatic flesh.

1.5 kg (3 lb 5 oz) greengage plums
750 g (1 lb 10 oz) sugar
juice of 1½ lemons

*Wash and sterilise seven 300 ml (10½ fl oz) jars (see page 10).*

Cut the fruit roughly in half near the stone and put it in a large nonreactive bowl or on a tray. Sprinkle the sugar over and toss to combine. Allow to macerate in the sugar in a cool place for an hour. It's not a bad idea to give it a toss a couple of times while it sits.

Tip this mixture, being sure to scrape out all the sugar and its juice, into a jam pan over high heat. Bring to the boil, then continue to cook over a reasonably high heat so it bubbles energetically, stirring often. Cook the plums for about 10–15 minutes until the fruit is softened and the jam has reached its setting point (see page 18).

Pass the jam through a sieve or mouli (to remove the stones) and transfer it straight into warmed jars, securing the lids immediately. This jam is a bit lower in sugar than most, so use it within about 6 months and it's best to store it in the fridge. For a shelf-stable jam, increase the sugar to equal weight of the pitted fruit and follow the recipe as above.

# BROWN SUGAR MARMALADE

MAKES ABOUT 3.3 KG (7 LB 6½ OZ)

900 g (2 lb) seville oranges

900 g (2 lb) sugar

900 g (2 lb) light brown sugar

2–3 tablespoons of a decent bourbon

Nicknamed Bitter & Twisted, this dark treacly marmalade is best served for breakfast, with black coffee and in silence. In the old days, a newspaper to read was the best accompaniment.

*Wash and sterilise twelve 300 ml (10½ fl oz) jars (see page 10).*

Wash the oranges and put them, whole, into a large saucepan with enough water to cover. Bring to the boil over high heat, then reduce the heat and simmer for 2 hours, until the skin is very soft.

Carefully scoop the oranges out of the liquid and set aside until they are cool enough to handle. Reserve the cooking liquid. Halve the oranges, scoop out the seeds and the membranes and tie them up in a muslin (cheesecloth) bag.

Quarter the orange peel halves and cut crossways into slices as thick as you like it.

Put the muslin bag into the saucepan with the orange cooking water. Bring the liquid to the boil over high heat and cook until reduced down to 1.5 litres (52 fl oz/6 cups).

Add the sliced peel and sugars and stir until the sugar has dissolved. If you have a jam pan, now is the time to use it. Return to the boil over high heat, spooning off any scum. Cook until setting point is reached, anywhere from 30 to 45 minutes (see page 18).

Remove from the heat, remove the muslin bag, giving it a good squeeze with a pair of tongs over the pan, then stir in a generous splash of decent bourbon. Pour into warmed jars, then seal and store in a cool, dark place for up to 2 years. Once opened, store in the fridge.

# THE QUINTESSENTIAL RASPBERRY JAM(S)

**MAKES ABOUT 1.8 KG (4 LB)**

A good raspberry jam is a really good jam. It's the perfect red jam and is an absolute favourite in our house. I've given two methods, one that creates an even textured jam; the other that leaves a few chunks. Both start out the same way, but finish differently. The important thing to remember is that raspberries aren't as good if cooked for more than about 12 minutes, because after that they start to lose quality (see page 16).

*Wash and sterilise six 300 ml (10½ fl oz) jars (see page 10).*

1 kg (2 lb 4 oz) raspberries

900g (2 lb) sugar, warmed gently in the oven

juice of 1 lemon, strained

## METHOD 1

Heat the raspberries with the warmed sugar (see page 17) and lemon juice in a wide-based pan, ideally a jam pan, over high heat. Stir it every minute or so using a flat-edge heatproof spatula (see page 16). After about 9 minutes start to test for a set (see page 18). Once set, remove the jam from the heat immediately, pour into warmed jars and seal with the lids immediately.

## METHOD 2

Heat half of the raspberries with the lemon juice and sugar in a jam pan over high heat for 8 minutes. Add the remaining fruit, bring to the boil again, cook for 2 minutes then check for the set (see page 18). Pour into warmed jars as above.

The jam should keep well for up to 2 years in the pantry. Store in the fridge once opened.

*Raspberry Jam*
recipe page 54

*Gentlemen's Marmalade*
recipe page 58

# GENTLEMEN'S MARMALADE
## (seville with whisky)

MAKES ABOUT 1.8 KG (4 LB)

You'll need to begin this recipe the day before. It's worth it, because the result is a tender, delightful, elegant marmalade of which Paddington Bear would be very approving.

1 kg (2 lb 4 oz) seville oranges

about 1 kg (2 lb 4 oz) sugar

a decent splash of whisky

**DAY 1** Halve the oranges and juice them. Collect the seeds and tie them up in a muslin (cheesecloth) sachet. Cut the juiced oranges into quarters, then use a sharp knife to carefully cut any remaining flesh and white pith away from the peel. Discard flesh and pith. Slice the orange peel as you like it: thin strips or chunky. Put the sliced peel in a large ceramic or other nonreactive bowl with the juice, the pip-filled muslin sachet and 1.5 litres (52 fl oz/6 cups) of water. Cover and leave in the fridge overnight.

**DAY 2** The next day, wash and sterilise six 300 ml (10¼ fl oz) jars (see page 10).

Pour the peel, liquid and muslin sachet into a jam pan over high heat. (If you have a copper jam pan, do this stage in a

*There are days, many days, when all I hanker for is a cup of tea and some hot buttered toast. Add marmalade, and it is always a good day.*

stainless steel saucepan, as it's only when you add sugar to the jam pan that it's considered food safe.) Bring to the boil, then reduce the heat and simmer on low for about 1½ hours until the peel is soft and you can squish it with your fingers.

Carefully remove the muslin bag, allow to cool slightly and squeeze any juice into the saucepan, as this is full of pectin, then discard the seeds and membranes.

Measure the liquid with the peel in it and add equal parts of sugar—500 g (1 lb 2 oz) of sugar to every 500 ml (17 fl oz/2 cups) of syrup—then return to the boil (now's the time you can—and should—use your copper jam pan). Reduce the heat slightly and keep the marmalade on a robust simmer for a further 30–40 minutes. Remove from the heat and check the set (see page 18). Add the whisky and stir through before pouring into sterilised jars.

Store the marmalade in the pantry for up to 2 years. Once it's opened, store it in the fridge.

# BARBARA'S CUMQUAT MARMALADE

MAKES ABOUT 2.5 KG (5 LB 8 OZ)

My mum, Barbara, has made a habit of preserving cumquats each year. She's not a prolific jam maker, or jam eater for that matter, but her marmalade has always been a treasured gift each time she comes to visit. And now, she's handed on her recipe for me to continue the tradition.

1 kg (2 lb 4 oz) cumquats, rinsed
1.2 kg (2 lb 10 oz) sugar

*Wash and sterilise nine 300 ml (10½ fl oz) jars (see page 10).*

Chop the cumquats and put them in a nonreactive bowl or a nonreactive pan you can make jam in. We tend to just cut the cumquats in quarters if they're small, but a finer cut peel is more to some people's liking. Barely cover the fruit with water and leave overnight to soak.

The next day, put the cumquats and soaking liquid in a jam pan over medium–high heat, add the sugar and bring to a simmer, stirring constantly while the sugar dissolves. Turn the heat right down and simmer until it reaches the set point (see page 18). This could take about 30 minutes, but it can be as little as 15 or as much as 40 minutes depending on the fruit and the heat and the shape of your pan.

You can skim off any seeds as it simmers, though we inevitably forget and they get caught in the finished marmalade. Which is just fine, really.

Transfer to warmed jars. Store in the pantry until opened, then store in the fridge. Use in a steamed pudding, or serve with hot buttered toast. Regularly.

# RHUBARB & ROSE JAM

**MAKES NEARLY 2 KG (4 LB 8 OZ)**

This is one time I really think you should use jam sugar or add pectin, as the rhubarb just struggles to get a nice set on its own. Don't worry if you don't have rose petals, you can stir in a little rosewater at the end just before bottling.

*Wash and sterilise about six 300 ml (10½ fl oz) jars (see page 10).*

Heat the rhubarb in a jam pan over medium heat with the sugar, lemon juice and vanilla bean, stirring while the sugar dissolves. Turn the heat to high and cook for about 10 minutes, stirring regularly, until a set is reached (see page 18).

Add the rose petals, cook for 1 minute more, then remove from the heat. If using rosewater, add just before bottling. Spoon into warmed jars, seal immediately, and store in the pantry for up to 1 year. Refrigerate after opening.

1 kg (2 lb 4 oz) rhubarb, trimmed and cut into 2 cm (¾ inch) lengths

1 kg (2 lb 4 oz) jam sugar, or sugar and 8 g (¼ oz) sachet of pectin, warmed (see page 17)

juice of 1 lemon, strained

1 vanilla bean, split lengthways

2 handfuls fragrant, unsprayed red rose petals (or use 2 teaspoons rosewater)

# ROASTED
# APRICOT JAM

**MAKES ABOUT 2 KG (4 LB 8 OZ)**

1.2 kg (2 lb 10 oz) apricots

770 g (1 lb 11 oz/3½ cups) sugar

30 g (1 oz) light brown sugar

60 ml (2 fl oz/¼ cup) strained
lemon juice

**If you want a basic apricot jam, try following the recipe for Greengage Jam on page 52 and simply replace the fruit. This one, however, has more caramel notes from the roasting, along with the complexity of brown sugar. Mixing the sugars makes the brown sugar far easier to sprinkle evenly.**

*Wash and sterilise seven 300 ml (10½ fl oz) jars (see page 10). Preheat the oven to 200°C (400°F).*

Halve the apricots and discard the stones. Lay the apricot halves, cut side up, on a baking tray, as close together as possible. Mix 30 g (1 oz) of the sugar with the brown sugar and sprinkle over evenly.

Roast the apricots for 20–40 minutes until they are browning on the edges. This time will vary a lot depending on the ripeness of your fruit.

Scrape the apricots and any juices into a jam pan or similar and add the remaining sugar and the lemon juice. Stir over low heat until the sugar has dissolved and the juices are running freely.

Increase the heat to medium and bring to a rolling boil. Keep stirring, as apricot jam is notorious for catching on the bottom of the pan.

After 20 minutes, check the set (see page 18). Pour into sterilised jars and store in a cool, dry, dark place for up to 2 years before using. Store opened jars in the fridge.

# GOOSEBERRY JAM

MAKES 2 KG (4 LB 8 OZ)

Every hill around us, if it didn't have apples on it, used to have small fruit on it. And many of those small fruit farms had gooseberries, which often ended up in jam. Well, it may have fallen out of favour, and so much jam may now be made with fruit from wherever, but the flavour of gooseberry jam is hard to beat. It's also, dare we say it, a great jam for beginners; almost foolproof because it has a decent pectin content and the fruit is a little harder to overcook than some. Once you've had some of this in the pantry, you'll be planting your own gooseberry bush just to be sure you always have a ready supply.

*Wash and sterilise seven 300 ml (10½ fl oz) jars (see page 10).*

Heat the gooseberries with 250 ml (9 fl oz/1 cup) of water in a jam pan (avoid copper pans as you're just softening the fruit at this stage and not adding sugar) over medium heat until it starts to simmer, then turn down the heat and cook the fruit gently for about 15 minutes until it softens. If you have a copper jam pan, transfer the mixture to the copper pan now. Add the lemon juice and sugar and stir to dissolve.

Turn the heat back to a rolling boil and cook until the jam reaches a set, checking after about 10 minutes (see page 18). It should take less than 20 minutes to reach a set. Some gooseberries can go a lovely ruby colour as they cook down.

Pour into sterilised jars, seal immediately and store in the pantry until opened. Once opened, store in the fridge

To make a cracking **Gooseberry & Elderflower Jam**, add about 3 tablespoons of elderflower cordial to the jam as soon as you take it off the stove.

1 kg (2 lb 4 oz) gooseberries, topped and tailed

juice of 1 lemon, strained

1 kg (2 lb 4 oz) sugar, warmed

# CHAPTER TWO: Jellies

A jelly is a curious thing. It's not got the bite and chew of jam. It doesn't linger in the mouth quite as long. But it does have a charm all its own, melting over meats, moistening a sandwich, puddling next to your roast lamb. It's a little bit of a teaser, adding elegance and subtlety, without the slap in the face of a thick conserve.

For us, a jelly is an art: the right texture is a source of pride. We use a few apples in the jelly oftentimes, to get a good set, because they're local and cheap and don't dominate other flavours. You can flavour jellies heavily, or not. You can make them barely set, or not. You can serve them with terrines, with good meats, use them to baste a roast leg of venison, or save them for dessert, depending on what you have in them.

The perfect set in your jelly is an elusive beast (see page 18). But don't fret, because even a loose or hard-set jelly has its uses, its own attraction, and the only people who don't make mistakes don't make anything. Making jelly is like life. It's a journey, not a destination. And the highs are extraordinarily high.

What's more, a few jars of jelly in the pantry are a sign of a discerning cook and a well-stocked kitchen.

# MINT JELLY

MAKES ABOUT 1 KG (2 LB 4 OZ)

1 kg (2 lb 4 oz) cooking apples
   (windfalls are good to use, too)
60 ml (2 fl oz/¼ cup) apple cider
   vinegar
500 g (1 lb 2 oz) sugar
generous bunch of mint, finely
   chopped

Homemade mint jelly is a cracker of a thing, the perfect foil for lamb. It's much better than any store-bought version and benefits from the lack of spooky green colouring.

*Wash and sterilise four 250 ml (9 fl oz/1 cup) jars (see page 10).*

**DAY 1** Roughly chop the apples: there is no need to remove any seeds or peel but cut out any bruised bits. Put the apple in a large saucepan and just cover with water; you'll need about 1 litre (35 fl oz/4 cups). Bring to the boil over high heat, then reduce the heat to a simmer and cook for about 1 hour, squashing the fruit with the back of a wooden spoon to help them break down, until the apples are soft.

Pour the mixture into a colander lined with muslin (cheesecloth) over a large bowl and leave to drip overnight.

**DAY 2** Measure the strained juice, which should be around 700 ml (24 fl oz). Put the measured juice into a preserving pan with the vinegar over medium heat, then add the sugar and stir until dissolved (adjust sugar accordingly if the yield isn't 700 ml). Increase the heat, bring to the boil and cook for about 10 minutes until setting point is reached (see page 18). Remove from the heat and stir the chopped mint through. Pour the jelly into warmed jars and seal. As the jelly cools, turn the jars upside down a few times so the mint doesn't get stuck at the top. Store in the pantry for up to a year, and in the fridge once opened.

# CRABAPPLE & PORT JELLY

**MAKES ABOUT 1.5 KG (3 LB 5 OZ)**

This fruit is beautiful to look at, like perfect blushing baby apples. Our favourite tree bursts forth in nearby Huonville and tempts young hands to test out the fruit, but, sadly, they're not very nice to eat raw. The good news is that there's always a few fruit left out of reach of little people, and a crabapple jelly is one of life's great joys to have in the pantry. Here's Fat Pig's version of the classic.

1.5 kg (3 lb 5 oz) crabapples
500 g (1 lb 2 oz) sugar
juice of 1 lemon, strained
100 ml (3½ fl oz) tawny (Port)

*Wash and sterilise three 500 ml (17 fl oz/2 cup) jars or similar (see page 10).*

Cut the crabapples in halves or quarters, leaving the peel on and cores in. Put them in a large stainless steel saucepan and cover with water. Cook for about 30 minutes until the fruit turns to a pulp.

Pour this mixture into a jelly bag, or a colander lined with two layers of muslin (cheesecloth), and allow to drain until all the juice has been extracted. Leave it overnight if you can. Don't be tempted to squeeze the pulp through, or your jelly will become cloudy.

Measure the juice into a preserving pan: you should have 1 litre (35 fl oz/4 cups). Warm the sugar in a low oven. Add the lemon juice to the pan and bring to boil then add the warm sugar. Reduce the heat and continue stirring until the sugar has dissolved. Increase the heat so that it starts to boil rapidly and leave to simmer for 8–10 minutes. Add the tawny and stir thoroughly.

Check the set (see page 18) and pour into sterilised jars immediately. Store in the pantry for up to a year, and in the fridge once opened.

# BLUEBERRY & BALSAMIC JELLY

**MAKES ABOUT 1.5 LITRES (52 FL OZ/6 CUPS)**

On one hand, blueberry jelly is forgiving because it's so dark you don't have to worry about cloudy jelly, but blueberries are low in pectin, so it can be tricky to get it to set. The white pith of a citrus contains lots of pectin, so I cut a thick slice off the end of a lemon and add it to the pan. Adding balsamic vinegar cuts through sweetness and lends a subtle depth to the flavour. If your jelly just doesn't set, stir the syrup through vanilla custard and churn to make a cracking blueberry ice cream.

1.8 kg (4 lb) fresh or frozen
  blueberries
1 kg (2 lb 4 oz) sugar
60 ml (2 fl oz/¼ cup) strained
  lemon juice
a thick slice of lemon
60 ml (2 fl oz/¼ cup) balsamic
  vinegar

*Wash and sterilise five or six 300 ml (10½ fl oz) jars (see page 10).*

Put the blueberries in a large saucepan and crush them slightly with a potato masher. Add 250 ml (9 fl oz/1 cup) of water, put it over very high heat and bring to the boil. Reduce the heat to medium and cook uncovered for 5 minutes.

Pour the berry mixture through a fine sieve and allow it to drain over a bowl for 1 hour. This should give you 1 litre (35 fl oz/4 cups) of blueberry juice.

Put this juice into a jam pan with the sugar, lemon juice, lemon slice and balsamic vinegar. Stir over medium heat until the sugar dissolves. Increase the heat to high and bring to the boil. The jelly will be a bit foamy at this point. Reduce the heat to medium but keep the jelly at a rolling boil. Give it a stir every now and then, but nothing too vigorous.

Keep up the rolling boil for about 15 minutes then remove from the heat and check the set (see page 18). If you let the jelly sit for a few moments you can skim off the scum before removing the lemon slice. Pour the jelly into sterilised jars and seal them. Store in the pantry for up to a year and then in the fridge once opened.

# QUINCE HONEY
**MAKES ABOUT 2 KG (4 LB 8 OZ)**

4 large quinces

1 kg (2 lb 4 oz) sugar

100 g (3½ oz) honey

1 thyme sprig

**This fragrant concoction is a kind of jelly, with its strips of quince melting into a sweet thick syrup. It's pretty much an item on its own, ready to woo you as a spread, but try it with a blue cheese or as a glaze for ham to see what is possible.**

*Wash and sterilise seven 300 ml (10½ fl oz) jars (see page 10).*

Quarter and core the quinces, leave the skin on and grate them coarsely.

Boil the sugar, honey and 300 ml (10½ fl oz) of water together in a large saucepan, removing any scum that appears on the surface. Add the grated quince and boil for 20 minutes. Skim if required. Remove from the heat, submerge the thyme into the quince honey mixture and allow to infuse for 10 minutes.

Remove the thyme (don't worry, a whole bunch of leaves will fall off, but it's the twigs you want to get out) and stir. Pour the quince honey into jars and seal.

Store in the pantry for up to a year, and in the fridge once it's opened.

*Medlar Jelly*
recipe page 78

*Medlar Jelly*
recipe page 78

# MEDLAR JELLY

MAKES ABOUT 1 KG (2 LB 4 OZ)

Cul-de-chien and open-arse are a couple of the other, perhaps more visceral, names for medlars; a strange looking fruit that is, ideally, bletted before use. Bletting is a process of rot, where the sugars increase and the tannin decreases. You can achieve the blet best by harvesting after a hard frost, and then letting the medlars sit at room temperature for a few weeks (ideally, on an absorbent paper or similar) until they go soft and brown, with a consistency a bit like a date. They make a delicious jelly that is perfect with chunky terrines, roast game or pork.

1.8 kg (4 lb) medlars, a mix of bletted and firm fruit

about 1 kg (2 lb 4 oz) sugar (exact amount will depend on yield from medlars)

1 cinnamon stick

juice of ½ lemon, strained

2 strips of lemon peel

*Wash and sterilise four 250 ml (9 fl oz/1 cup) jars (see page 10).*

**DAY 1** Cut the fruit into quarters, which will be messy if they've bletted properly, and put it in a stainless steel saucepan. Just cover the fruit with water and bring to the boil. Cook the medlars until soft. Pour into a colander lined with muslin (cheesecloth), set it over a jug and leave to drip overnight. You could even use a jelly bag (see page 16), but they're not essential. Don't be tempted to squeeze the pulp or you will have a cloudy jelly.

**DAY 2** Measure the medlar juice. For every 600 ml (21 fl oz) of juice allow 450 g (1 lb) of sugar. This is a variation on an old jelly-maker's ratio—a pint (of liquid) to a pound (of sugar)—but it's not so catchy when converted to metric.

Heat the juice in a jam pan or similar and warm the sugar in a low oven, then add to the hot juice. Add the cinnamon stick, lemon juice and peel. Bring to the boil, stirring until the sugar is dissolved then continue to gently boil for about 40 minutes until setting point is reached (see page 18). Pour into the prepared jars and seal. Store in the pantry for up to a year, and in the fridge once open.

NOT JUST JAM

# BLACKBERRY & APPLE JELLY

**MAKES ABOUT 1.2 KG (2 LB 10 OZ)**

1 kg (2 lb 4 oz) cooking apples, washed

200 g (7 oz) blackberries

about 1 kg (2 lb 4 oz) sugar

Sweet and heady with the autumn harvest, this is heaven passed through a jelly bag. Like all jellies, you have to drain it overnight, so plan ahead and start it on a Saturday so it's done by the end of the weekend.

*Wash and sterilise four 300 ml (10½ fl oz) jars (see page 10).*

**DAY 1** Chop the apples, skin and core and all, roughly. Put the apple in a large saucepan with just enough water to cover. Cook over high heat, bring to the boil then turn down to a simmer and cook until softened, squashing the pieces with the back of a wooden spoon to help them break down. This will take about 1 hour: when the apples are soft, they're ready.

Add the blackberries and continue cooking for another 10 minutes or so, just to soften the fruit.

Strain the fruit through a jelly bag (see page 16) overnight.

**DAY 2** Discard the solids from the jelly bag, and measure the amount of liquid. Put the liquid in a clean saucepan or jam pan. For every 100 ml (3½ fl oz) of juice add 60 g (2¼ oz) of sugar. Bring to the boil over high heat, then turn to a slightly more moderate heat (a good rolling boil is best) until it reaches a nice jelly set (see page 18).

Pour into the warmed jars and store in the pantry until opened, then store in the fridge.

This jelly is superb melting into crumpets, on yummy things like waffles or it can even be used to glaze fruit flans. I've been known to eat it out of the jar with just a spoon, though it does taste better with a bit of whipped cream for company.

# SLOE & APPLE JELLY

MAKES ABOUT 2 KG (4 LB 8 OZ)

1 kg (2 lb 4 oz) apples, washed

1 kg (2 lb 4 oz) sloes, rinsed

about 1 kg (2 lb 4 oz) sugar

We adore the flavour of the berries from the blackthorn, which are called sloes. They grow on hedgerows around Tassie, though most are in the north, not where we live. They're a bit tricky to pick—the sharp thorns make for the occasional pierced hand—but a good thicket will provide a kilo's harvest in quick time. For some uses, such as sloe gin, it's important that the sloes are well frosted, but because we're boiling them in this you don't have to bother. Frozen sloes work better because the unfrosted, unfrozen type are a bit firm to cook.

*Wash and sterilise seven 300 ml (10½ fl oz) jars (see page 10).*

Chop the apples, skin, core and all, roughly. Put the apple pieces and sloes in a large saucepan with just enough water to cover. Heat it over high heat, bring to the boil then turn down to a simmer and cook until the fruit is softened, squashing the sloes as you go if they aren't softening and breaking down readily. This will take about 1 hour: don't worry about overcooking them, with this recipe it's hard to overcook the fruit.

Strain the fruit through a jelly bag (see page 16) or muslin (cheesecloth), discard the solids, and measure the amount of liquid you get. Place the liquid in a clean saucepan or jam pan. For every 100 ml (3½ fl oz) of juice add 100 g (3½ oz) of sugar. Heat over high heat, bring to the boil then reduce to a slightly more moderate heat (a good rolling boil is best) until it reaches a nice jelly set (see page 18).

Pour into sterilised jars and store in the pantry until opened, then store in the fridge. Sloe and apple jelly is great with game, lamb, terrines and the like. It's even delicious with some hard cheeses and pretty damn fine with brie.

# CHAPTER THREE:

# Preserves.

W hen I first moved to Tasmania, elongated pears fell from the ancient tree onto the roof of the flat I was renting in Hobart. Appalled by the thought of them simply rotting, I scoured the op shops for Fowlers jars, the iconic Australian preserving jars, and found plenty. I filled every last one of them with pears, some flavoured with spices, others not, and suddenly I'd joined the ranks of fruit preservers, almost by accident. A happy accident, because I ate the resultant fruit for nearly two years after; jaunty bottles of nude pink-coloured pears steeped in a light syrup.

Preserving is an art (see page 20), but also an inexact science, where a home preserve is better than the glut of the season gone to waste or, heaven forbid, tinned fruit. Most of the recipes are for minimal amounts, but we tend to do a much larger quantity and find any jars we can that are shaped to suit the fruit.

Be sure to find a use for the syrup in the bottles as well, because it has trapped so much of the flavour of the fruit. Add a little more sugar and serve it as you would any fruit syrup.

# PEARS WITH SAFFRON & MACE

**MAKES ABOUT 1.8 KG (4 LB)**

Around us, enormous old pear trees dot the landscape and in autumn they are laden with fruit. Most of these pears aren't great to eat fresh, rather they're designed to preserve. If you're buying fruit, look out for slightly under-ripe fruit and varieties such as beurre bosc, which stay firmer when cooked.

*Wash and sterilise four 750 ml (26 fl oz/3 cup) preserving jars or similar (see page 10).*

Peel and quarter the pears and keep them in a big bowl of water to prevent them browning too much as you work. Cut out the cores and place the pears in preserving jars, trying to jiggle them in between each other so the jar is packed tightly. Add 1 tablespoon of sugar to each jar, along with a small pinch of saffron and 2 blades of mace. Fill each jar with water, up to about 1 cm (⅜ inch) from the top. Seal the jars and stand them in a preserving pan or a tall saucepan that can have its lid on after the jars are in. Pour water in with the jars to come at least three-quarters of the way up the sides of the jars, or even further.

Bring to the boil over medium heat. Put on the lid and turn the heat down to a bare simmer, then cook for 35 minutes. Remove the lid and, when you are able, remove the jars from the water.

Store in a cool, dark place, such as a pantry or cellar. Preserved fruit can keep for a couple of years without losing quality.

2 kg (4 lb 8 oz) pears

about 4 tablespoons sugar

4 pinches of saffron threads

8 mace blades

# BRANDY-PRESERVED CHERRIES

**MAKES 1 KG (2 LB 4 OZ)**

Preserved cherries make a fresh, summery gift that friends will be able to treasure long after the fleeting cherry season is over.

*Wash and sterilise four 250 ml (9 fl oz/1 cup) preserving jars (see page 10).*

To make the syrup, bring 300 ml (10¼ fl oz) of water and the sugar to the boil in a large saucepan over medium heat, stirring to dissolve the sugar. Add the cassia bark and nutmeg once it's boiling, reduce the heat to low and simmer for 15 minutes. Add the brandy and cherries and simmer, stirring occasionally, for 15 minutes.

Transfer to warmed jars, seal and store in a cool, dark place, preferably for a month, before using.

300 g (10½ oz/1⅓ cups firmly packed) brown sugar

2 pieces cassia bark

1 whole nutmeg, cracked into 2 pieces

300 ml (10½ fl oz) brandy or kirsch

1 kg (2 lb 4 oz) white cherries, (or sour or other cherries), pitted (if you're feeling up to it)

# CUMQUATS
# IN BRANDY

MAKES 500 G (1 LB 2 OZ) CUMQUATS, PLUS THE SCENTED BRANDY

500 g (1 lb 2 oz) cumquats

2 tablespoons sugar

about 500 ml (17 fl oz/2 cups)
    brandy or similar

a year of your life

I grew up with these. A strange, tall bottle of cumquats, slowly leaching colour into their soaking liquid, high on a kitchen shelf. Mum used to just gobble one down every now and then, or use them in desserts for her dinner parties, relishing the zesty character. When I tasted one at age 12 or so, with its tang and bitterness and high alcohol, I thought it was the devil's work. Times have changed.

*Wash well a 1 litre (35 fl oz/4 cup) tall jar or similar. There's no real need to sterilise it, because of the alcohol content, but it's not a bad idea if you're up for it (see page 10).*

Wash the cumquats well and place them in the jar. Ideally, you'd use something that can be on display. Whisk the sugar into the brandy and pour it on top of the fruit. Seal well, and leave for a year or so before consuming, and using the brandy in desserts.

# VANILLA PEACHES

**MAKES ABOUT 900 G (2 LB)**

Small peaches and nectarines are simple to preserve as they fit in jars more easily. They need a shorter cooking time than some fruit, such as pears, because they're delicate in nature. There are two distinct types of peach flesh: melting flesh, which (when ripe) seemingly melts as you bite into one (over the bath!); and rubber flesh (or firm flesh, or nonmelting). The latter, while not as good to eat fresh, preserve really well, though both can be bottled with success.

*Wash and sterilise two 750 ml (26 fl oz/3 cup) preserving jars (see page 10).*

Cut the peaches in half and remove the stones. If they're large, you may want to cut them in quarters. Gently ease them into the preserving jars, packing them as tightly as you can without bruising the fruit. Experienced preservers can make really neat stacks of halved fruit, but it's just as nice to eat if they're not neat, though you may need more jars if you can't get the fruit to sit nicely on top of each other.

Add a tablespoon of sugar and half the vanilla bean to each jar. Fill with water to 1 cm (⅜ inch) below the top. Don't overfill, but do try to jiggle and poke the fruit so that there are no air bubbles that will cause the water level to drop. Seal with the lids. Stand the jars in a preserving pan or a tall saucepan with a lid. Fill it with water that comes at least three-quarters of the way up the sides of the jars, cover the pan and bring to the boil over medium heat. Reduce the heat to low and simmer gently for 25 minutes.

When the jars are cool enough to handle, remove them from the pan and allow to cool completely before storing them for up to 12 months in the pantry.

1 kg (2 lb 4 oz) peaches

2 tablespoons sugar

1 vanilla bean, cut in half lengthways

# BLOOD PLUMS WITH RED WINE & CLOVES

**MAKES 1 KG (2 LB 4 OZ)**

Preserved plums have a lovely richness, here enhanced with the use of red wine. As they age, they tend to get darker in colour, which isn't a bad thing. We use leftover wine for preserves like this, and if it's a big, bold wine, like shiraz or cabernet, we might nudge up the sugar content slightly. The amount in this recipe, however, makes them just as good for some savoury uses as dessert.

1 kg (2 lb 4 oz) blood plums, or other red European style plums
2 tablespoons brown sugar
200 ml (7 fl oz) red wine
4 whole cloves

*Clean and sterilise four 500 ml (17 fl oz/2 cup) preserving jars (see page 10). The ideal shape will depend a bit on the size of the plums.*

Place the plums in the jars, gently easing them in between each other so they pack as tightly in the jars as possible without squashing them out of shape completely.

Distribute the sugar evenly among the jars (if it's four jars, it'll take 2 teaspoons per jar), do the same with the wine (2½ tablespoons per jar) and the cloves. Top the jars up with water, seal them well, and stand them in a preserving pan or a large saucepan (see page 20). Add water to the pan to come three-quarters of the way up the sides of the jars.

Bring the water to the boil over medium heat, cover if need be according to the type of preserving pan you're using, and simmer for 25 minutes. If you have tongs for removing hot jars from the water, use those to take the jars out and stand them on a wooden surface (a marble, stone or even steel bench can be cold and could crack the jars). Cool completely, then store in the pantry for up to 2 years before using. Once open, they have the properties of poached fruit so need to be stored in the fridge and used within a few days.

# CINNAMON-SPICED NECTARINES WITH WHITE WINE

MAKES 1 KG (2 LB 4 OZ)

1 kg (2 lb 4 oz) nectarines

2 cinnamon sticks

200 ml (7 fl oz) white wine

2 tablespoons sugar

Sometimes, a little extra spice in the preserving jars adds a whole other character. Add a little wine, too, and the result is a fruit that tastes completely different to the standard preserves. Here, the sweet aroma of cinnamon and the tartness of white wine combine with the fragrance of nectarines to produce a lovely combination worthy of the best homemade vanilla ice cream.

*Wash and sterilise two 750 ml (26 fl oz/3 cup) preserving jars or similar (see page 10).*

Cut the nectarines in half and remove the stones. Slide the cut halves into the jars, trying to stack them neatly on top of each other so they pack the jars as tightly as possible without mangling or bruising the fruit. You can buy tools that help with this, or a chopstick is kinda handy, too.

Add a cinnamon stick, 100 ml (3½ fl oz) of wine and a tablespoon of sugar to each jar. Fill with water to about 1 cm (⅜ inch) from the top, jiggling the fruit to ensure there are minimal bubbles caught underneath. Cap and seal the jars.

Stand the jars in a preserving pan or similar, cover with a lid and bring to the boil over medium heat. Turn the heat down to a simmer and cook for 25 minutes. Remove from the heat, take off the lid and, when you're able, take the jars from the pan and stand them on a wooden chopping board to cool completely. The nectarines will store for up to 2 years in a cool, dark pantry.

# APRICOTS WITH ORANGE BLOSSOM & NUTMEG

MAKES ABOUT 900 G (2 LB)

Apricots, if picked ripe, can become very tender when preserved, to the point of falling apart. Fret not, because the flavour remains the same and a bottle (or five) in the pantry is a treasure worth discovering every time you need a little summer fruit in midwinter.

1 kg (2 lb 4 oz) apricots

2 tablespoons sugar

½ nutmeg, cracked into two pieces

2 teaspoons orange blossom water

*Wash and sterilise two 750 ml (26 fl oz/3 cup) preserving jars or similar (see page 10).*

Halve the apricots and remove the stones. Pack the fruit into the jars, jiggling them to get them to sit closely and neatly together. This packing is a real art, and one I'm only now learning. If you have a granny or someone close who has experience, get them to give you a couple of lessons.

Spoon 1 tablespoon of sugar into each jar. Add a chunk of nutmeg and a teaspoon of orange blossom water to each one. Pour in enough cold water to come to 1 cm (⅜ inch) from the top. Use a chopstick to help get air bubbles out from between the fruit and up to the top, tipping the jar from side to side as need be.

Seal the jars, stand them in a tall saucepan or preserving pan that is big enough so you can put the lid on with the jars inside. Pour in enough water to come at least three-quarters of the way up the side of each jar. Pop on the lid, put it over medium heat and bring to the boil. Turn the heat down to a low simmer and cook for about 25 minutes. Remove from the heat, take off the lid and, when cool enough to handle with a cloth, remove the jars from the water.

When the jars have cooled completely, store them in the pantry. They'll keep for up to 2 years if stored correctly.

# CHAPTER FOUR:
# Pickles + Relishes

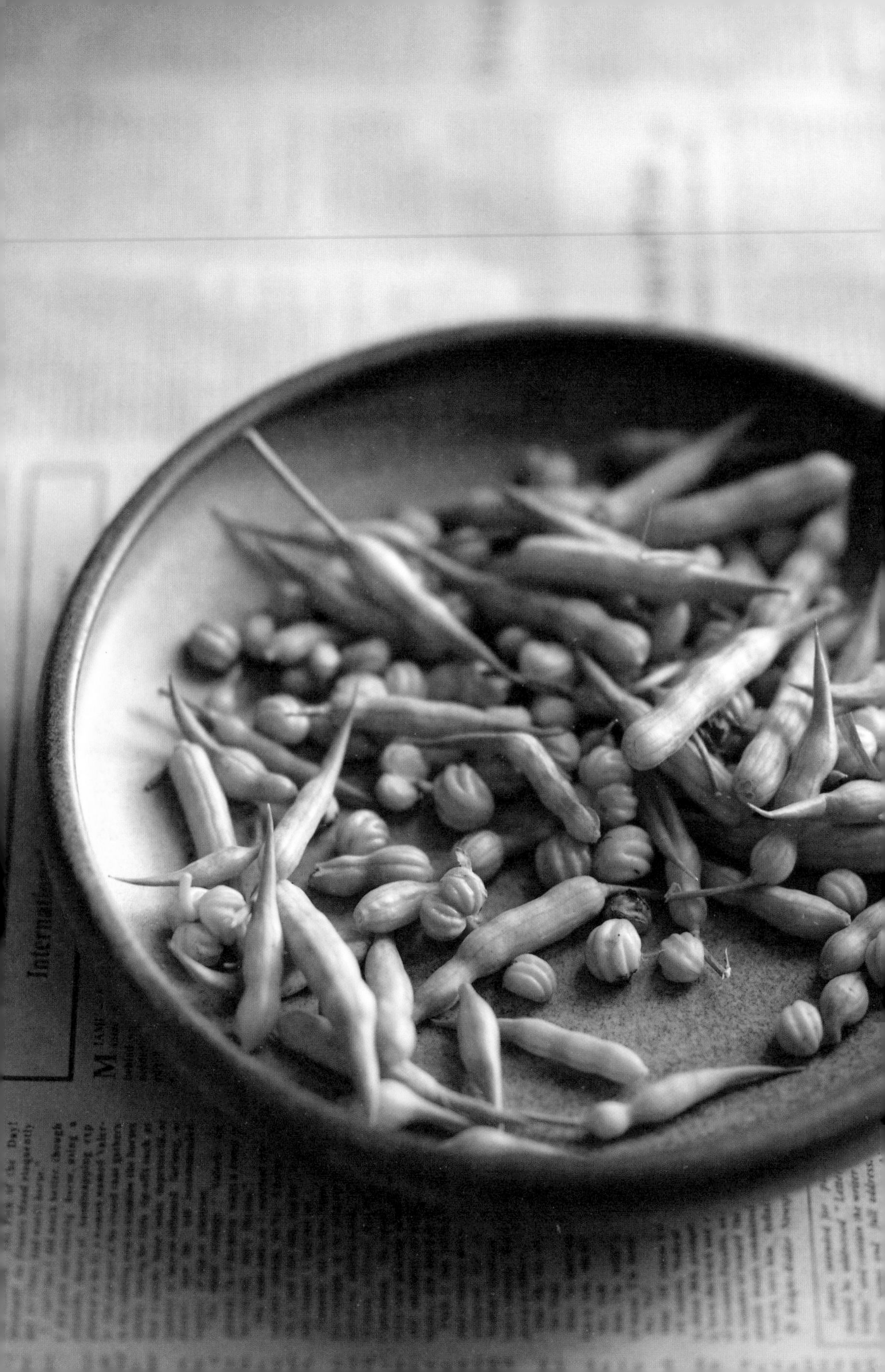

So, you need something to jazz up a meal, do you? To add interest to a particularly boring cheese sandwich? A great mustard to match your great corned beef? Or a piccalilli for which everybody will ask about the recipe, because it's not just edible (unlike some, in my opinion), it's incredible.

Well, this is the chapter that will make your pantry come alive. It's the go-to place that can liven up a curry (the Lime Pickle), lift your leftover roast lamb to great heights (the Lemon Chutney), embellish your picky plate (what we call a ploughman's equivalent of what's good in the fridge), or make your Christmas ham even more divine.

These are the essentials—this is the chapter—of everyday, ordinary pickles and relishes that will make every meal better than ordinary. These are the kinds of things you make a big batch of so you can give the surplus to your friends. A treasure trove of good things, laid down for times when you still want to eat well, but may not have the chance to cook.

# DILL PICKLED CUCUMBERS

**MAKES 600 G (1 LB 5 OZ)**

We've grown a handful of tiny cucumbers, the sort that look like gherkins, but mostly we're more successful with bigger cucumbers such as the Lebanese ones that are a bit bigger than a man's thumb. These, when sliced, make a terrific pickle that really goes well with corned beef or pastrami, though it's also a cracker with cheese.

*Wash and sterilise two 500 ml (17 fl oz/2 cup) jars (see page 10).*

In a large nonreactive (glass, ceramic or plastic) bowl, toss the cucumber with the onion, salt and hot water and set aside for 3 hours. Drain, reserving the liquid.

In a medium saucepan, pop the vinegar, sugar, mustard seeds, dill, turmeric and chilli (if using). Bring to the boil over high heat, add the cucumber and its soaking liquid then reduce the heat to low and simmer for 2 minutes. Transfer the pickles to sterilised jars. Store for a month, ideally, before using, to let flavours develop.

600 g (1 lb 5 oz) Lebanese (short) cucumbers, very thinly sliced

1 brown onion, thinly sliced

1½ tablespoons salt

60 ml (2 fl oz/¼ cup) hot water

250 ml (9 fl oz/1 cup) white wine vinegar

200 g (7 oz) sugar

2 teaspoons brown mustard seeds

2–3 tablespoons chopped dill

¼ teaspoon ground turmeric

chilli flakes (optional)

# DARK BROWN PICKLE

**MAKES A BIT OVER 2 KG (4 LB 8 OZ)**

1 onion, about 100 g (3½ oz), diced

2 swedes (rutabagas), about 500 g (1 lb 2 oz), peeled and finely diced

1 large carrot, about 150 g (5½ oz), peeled and finely diced

6 garlic cloves, finely chopped

6 dates, about 115 g (4 oz), roughly chopped

½ head cauliflower, finely chopped

2 apples, peeled, cored and diced

500 g (1 lb 2 oz) dark brown sugar

100 ml (3½ fl oz) lemon juice

250 ml (9 fl oz/1 cup) apple cider vinegar

125 ml (4 fl oz/½ cup) Worcestershire Sauce (see page 142)

2 teaspoons mustard seeds

¼ teaspoon ground allspice

½ teaspoon cayenne pepper

1 teaspoon ground coriander

1 teaspoon ground cinnamon

90 g (3¼ oz/¼ cup) molasses

1 tablespoon salt

I used to think I didn't like pickles. Until I was travelling as a teenager in the UK, that is, insatiably hungry, hitching rides around the countryside and trying to fill up on ploughman's lunches at the local pubs. It was there that I discovered a dark pickle (a particularly famed version is Branston Pickle) that started a love affair with good pickles thereafter. I still adore this style with cheddar cheese, though it's great with other things, too; even a rustic terrine or on a roast beef sandwich, or with pork sausages and onion.

*Wash and sterilise eight 300 ml (10½ fl oz) jars (see page 10).*

Combine all of the ingredients with 150 ml (5 fl oz) of water in a large saucepan, stirring over medium heat until the sugar has dissolved. Bring to a gentle simmer and cook for 45 minutes, stirring occasionally until the vegetables are coated in a good thick sauce. You want the vegetables to still have some texture. Carefully spoon the mixture into warmed sterile jars, seal immediately, and store in a cool, dark place for at least a month, and up to six months, or even longer. Keep in the fridge once open.

# A GARDENER'S
## (*and edible*) PICCALILLI

**MAKES ABOUT 3 KG (6 LB 12 OZ)**

I must say, I've always been a bit underwhelmed by ordinary store-bought piccalilli: the one with corn and capsicum in it, the sort that's one-dimensional with turmeric and cheap vinegar. The thing about a good piccalilli is that it is a celebration of the garden. Don't, please, put corn in it. Just some great vegetables, heavy on the cauliflower, and fragrant with a little spice. If you have cucumber, or a marrow (squash) of some kind, you can add that. Some green tomatoes? Yes, please. Radish pods from some plants that you won't be harvesting the seeds? Perfect. You're aiming at about 2 kg (4 lb 8 oz) of vegetables in total.

*Wash and sterilise six 500 ml (17 fl oz/2 cup) jars (see page 10).*

Toss all the vegetables (including the radish pods and nasturtium seeds) with the salt in a large, nonreactive (glass, ceramic or plastic) bowl and let it stand overnight. The next day, rinse the salt off and drain well.

Mix the mustard powder, spices and flour together with a few tablespoons of vinegar to make a smooth paste, then whisk in the remainder of the vinegar and the celery seeds. Pour this mixture into a medium saucepan, pop it over medium–high heat and bring to the boil, stirring pretty much constantly. When it comes to the boil, turn it down to a simmer and, stirring often, simmer for 10 minutes.

When that's done, whisk the sugar into the sauce then stir this mixture well through the vegetables and put the mixture into warmed jars. Tighten the lids, and leave them in the pantry a good month or two before eating. Once open, store in the fridge or consume within 2 weeks.

400 g (14 oz) green tomatoes (about 2), diced

400 g (14 oz) brown onions (about 2), peeled and diced

800 g (1 lb 12 oz) cauliflower, cut into tiny florets, stems included

1 zucchini (courgette), diced

1 carrot, grated or finely shredded

½ cup radish pods, sliced crossways (optional)

40 g (1½ oz/4 tablespoons) nasturtium seeds

2 tablespoons fine salt

2 tablespoons dried mustard powder

2 tablespoons ground turmeric

2 tablespoons ground ginger

2 tablespoons plain (all-purpose) flour

1.2 litres (42 fl oz) white wine vinegar

2 teaspoons celery seeds

4 tablespoons brown sugar

## ❧ RADISH PODS ❧

*Radish pods and nasturtium seeds are a gardener's luxury. If you have them, use them. Otherwise simply omit them and use another vegetable instead.*

# PICKLED TOMATILLOS

**MAKES 1 KG (2 LB 4 OZ)**

Tomatillos are amazingly good, but they're far better once cooked or pickled. Even better, if they're pickled you can eat them all year. Try this with fresh tomatillos, and then try chargrilling them for a completely different flavour profile.

*Wash and sterilise three 300 ml (10½ fl oz) jars (see page 10).*

Remove the papery husk from the tomatillos, cut into quarters and pack them into jars.

To make the pickling solution, put the rest of ingredients in a medium saucepan over high heat and bring to the boil, then turn down and simmer for 10 minutes. Remove the chillies if you don't want your pickles too spicy, or leave them in for a bit more kick. Pour the pickling solution over the tomatillos and seal the jars. Allow to mellow for at least 1 week before cracking open the jar, though a bit longer is better. Store in the pantry, and in the fridge once opened.

500 g (1 lb 2 oz) tomatillos
1 or 2 small red or green chillies
2 garlic cloves, sliced
1 teaspoon coriander seeds
250 ml (9 fl oz/1 cup) apple cider
  vinegar
250 ml (9 fl oz/1 cup) water
3 teaspoons salt

# BEETROOT RELISH

**MAKES 2 KG (4 LB 8 OZ)**

a splash of olive oil

1 tablespoon yellow mustard seeds

2 brown onions, finely diced

1 kg (2 lb 4 oz) beetroot (beets),
peeled and grated

5 cm (2 inch) piece of horseradish,
peeled and grated

2 teaspoons salt

1 teaspoon freshly ground
black pepper

4 strips of orange peel, taken with
a potato peeler

500 ml (17 fl oz/2 cups) apple
cider vinegar

300 g (10½ oz) brown sugar

200 g (7 oz) sugar

We love our beetroot in Australia. On burgers, in salads, with the barbecue, in fact just about everywhere except breakfast. This relish works for most of those uses, too, and is ready at a moment's notice. Try it on a steak sanger, to lift a burger, with skewered lamb or as an accompaniment to saganaki or other melted cheesy things.

*Wash and sterilise three 500 ml (17 fl oz/2 cup) jars (see page 10).*

Heat the olive oil over medium heat in a large saucepan and add the mustard seeds, stirring until they begin to pop. Working quickly so the seeds don't burn, add the onion, turn down the heat to very low and cook until the onion begins to soften, but not colour; you want them translucent.

Add the remaining ingredients to the pan and stir over medium heat until the sugar has dissolved. Turn up the heat, bring to the boil, then turn down to a simmer and cook for about 1 hour, stirring occasionally until the beetroot is soft and the mixture is jammy. Fish out the orange peel, fill warmed jars with the relish and seal. Store in a cool, dark place for up to a year and pop into the fridge once the jar is opened.

# INDIAN-STYLE SALTED LIME PICKLE

**MAKES 400 G (14 OZ)**

When I first met my partner, Sadie, she didn't let on that her family recipe for salted lime pickle was a thing of wonder. It was only after I wooed her for a few months that a small, unassuming jar of pickle was brought from the fridge and delivered with characteristic understatement. In it, I found a perfect accompaniment to curries. And now that the secret is out, Fat Pig Farm is happy to share the recipe with you, too.

400 g (14 oz) limes
1½ tablespoons salt
1 teaspoon ground turmeric
½ teaspoon cayenne pepper
2 teaspoons ground allspice
about 2–3 tablespoons white vinegar

*Wash and sterilise several 200–300 ml ( 7–10½ fl oz) jars (see page 10).*

Make this when limes are cheap. Dice the limes, discarding the seeds, into about 1 cm (⅜ inch) pieces, reserving any juice. Carefully pack the flesh into sterile jars. Combine the salt, spices, vinegar and lime juice and pour into the jars over the limes. Seal. Stand the jars in a warm spot, even with a little sunlight, for a week or so. It's important to jiggle the limes often to keep the liquid around them. Once they've softened, store them in the pantry (or a cool, dark spot) for 6 months before using.

# GREEN TOMATO RELISH

**MAKES 1.5 KG (3 LB 5 OZ)**

Like most gardens, ours often leaves us with a few green tomatoes each autumn that just aren't going to ripen. Hence, the need for a good, reliable relish to make with the crop. This one has a little warmth from mustard and cayenne, a pulpy character from the apple, and the occasional sultana for sparkle. Use it under melted cheese on a toastie, with corned beef or ham, with pastrami, or as an accompaniment to a dangerously good meatloaf.

*Wash and sterilise six 300 ml (10½ fl oz) jars (see page 10).*

Put the tomato, onion and apple in a large saucepan over low heat with half the vinegar, and cook for about 30 minutes until the apples are soft and falling apart. The tomato should be soft by this stage, too. Add the rest of the vinegar and the remaining ingredients, and simmer for 10–15 minutes until the mixture thickens, stirring occasionally to avoid it catching on the bottom of the pan.

Spoon into warmed, sterile jars, cap immediately, cool, and then store in a cool, dark place for 1 month prior to using. Once opened, store in the fridge.

1 kg (2 lb 4 oz) green tomatoes, stem ends removed, chopped

2 large brown onions, diced

1 large cooking apple, such as granny smith, peeled, cored and chopped

300 ml (10½ fl oz) malt vinegar

100 g (3½ oz) sultanas (golden raisins)

2 teaspoons salt

½ teaspoon cayenne pepper

1 teaspoon mustard powder

100 g (3½ oz) sugar

# PICKLED GARLIC SCAPES

**MAKES 500 G (1 LB 2 OZ)**

500 g (1 lb 2 oz) garlic scapes

500 ml (17 fl oz/2 cups) apple
cider vinegar

250 ml (9 fl oz/1 cup) water

2 tablespoons salt

1 tablespoon sugar

1 tablespoon whole black
peppercorns

½ teaspoon mustard seeds

A 'scape' is the botanical name for a leafless stalk
that grows directly from the ground, so it's the perfect
name for the long, curved stalk of the garlic flower.
In spring when last year's garlic stash is finished
and the summer harvest is a few months off, we snip
off the scapes to help bridge the gap when the garlic
cupboard is bare. Pickled, they bring their joy into
other seasons, too.

*Wash and sterilise two 400 ml (14 fl oz) jars (see page 10).*

Trim the pointy end off the flower tip, which is rather tough
and chewy, along with the dry end of the scape. If you test
the end for bendiness, you can check where the softer part
of the stem begins. Trim from that point.

Pack the trimmed scapes into sterile jars. I like to coil the
long scapes around the inside of the jars, but you can trim
them into shorter lengths if you prefer. Warm the base of the
jars in warm water so they don't crack when you add the hot
liquid pickle.

Now get cracking on the pickling solution. Put the remaining
ingredients into a medium saucepan over very high heat and
bring to the boil, stirring until the sugar and salt is dissolved.
Pour over the scapes and seal the jars immediately. Store
in the fridge and open after a minimum of 2 weeks, ideally
a month later.

# PICKLED TURNIPS

**MAKES 800 G (1 LB 12 OZ)**

This is a Middle Eastern classic, the perfect addition to a falafel roll or similar. It's also a pickle that we've adopted, because turnips grow so well here, and this is a delicious way to preserve them. The small amount of beetroot stains the pickling solution pink. Turnips have never looked so pretty.

*Wash and sterilise a 2 litre (70 fl oz/8 cup) jar (see page 10) or equivalent.*

Wash the turnips studiously and cut them into quarters. Peel the garlic cloves and give them a gentle bash with the flat of a knife. Peel the beetroot and cut it into small wedges.

It's best to get a nice big jar for this, about 2 litres in size. Layer the turnips into the jar, tucking in the garlic cloves and beetroot wedges here and there as you go. Warm the base of the jar to avoid it cracking as you do the next bit. Set the jar aside and get on with the pickling solution.

Combine the vinegar and salt with 500 ml (17 fl oz/2 cups) of water in a medium saucepan and stir over medium heat until the salt has dissolved. Bring to the boil. Remove from the heat and pour the solution into the turnip-filled jar. Seal and leave in a dark cupboard for 7 days at least. Once opened, keep in the fridge and use within a month.

The turnips are fantastic with cured meats, such as pastrami or ham, with cheeses, on a ploughman's platter, with pâté or terrine, as well as on a falafel roll.

| |
|---|
| 750 g (1 lb 10 oz) turnips: little white ones work best |
| 2 large garlic cloves |
| 1 small beetroot (beet), about 60 g (2¼ oz) |
| 250 ml (9 fl oz/1 cup) white wine vinegar |
| 3 teaspoons salt |

# PICKLED ONIONS

**MAKES 1 KG (2 LB 4 OZ)**

1 kg (2 lb 4 oz) peeled pickling
   onions
boiling water, to cover
100 g (3½ oz) salt

**PICKLING JUICE**

1 litre (35 fl oz/4 cups) apple cider
   or malt vinegar
1 teaspoon juniper berries
1 teaspoon whole black
   peppercorns
3 fresh bay leaves
2 tablespoons dark brown sugar

**The ideal onions for this are small and firm. You
can pickle French shallots in this mixture, too,
or replace the dark brown sugar with honey for
a different end result.**

*Wash and sterilise two 1 litre (35 fl oz/4 cup) jars (see page 10)
or equivalent, depending on size of onions.*

Put the onions in a large heatproof container. Pour over
enough boiling water to cover, whisk in the salt and let the
onions steep in this liquid until cool. Maybe lay a plate over
the top to keep them all submerged if necessary, and then
leave overnight if possible.

Pop all the pickling juice ingredients into a medium
saucepan and bring to the boil. Simmer for 5 minutes.

Drain the onions and drop them into the jars, being sure to
leave enough room at the top for the pickling juice to cover
them. Warm the base of the jars carefully in a water bath so
you don't crack the jars from temperature shock as you do
the next stage. Carefully pour the hot pickling liquid over the
onions in the jars, enough to cover, and put the lids on firmly.
Cool well and store in a cool, dark place, such as a pantry, for
at least a month before opening. They're better after a couple
of months really, and they keep well for up to 2 years. Store in
the fridge once opened.

# PARKS'S LEMON CHUTNEY

**MAKES ABOUT 1.6 KG (3 LB 8 OZ/6 CUPS)**

My wife's late father, Parks Chrestman, used to make a few things for the family, including Lime Pickle (page 110), tomato sauce (Newlands Sauce, page 134) and this lemon chutney. Apparently he used to get a bit lazy with the chutney, leaving it just a little long between stirs, so it caught on the bottom and darkened dangerously in spots. This, apparently, is the secret method that marks the difference between a good chutney and a great one; some inattention is required.

*Wash and sterilise five 300 ml (10½ fl oz) jars (see page 10).*

Put the lemon pieces and onion in a large bowl, toss with the salt and leave to stand overnight.

The next day, put the lemon and onion and all their juices in a large stainless steel pan with about 125 ml (4 fl oz/½ cup) of water and simmer until soft. Add the remaining ingredients, bring back to the boil and then turn the heat right down to a simmer. Cook until it is a nice thick consistency, for about 30 minutes minimum, stirring occasionally. It could take 1½ hours or a tad longer. Sadie reckons you have to forget it a bit so you scorch the bottom and give the chutney way more character. I, of course, always obey.

Pour into jars and store in the pantry, or in the fridge once opened. It's simply amazing on lamb sandwiches.

6 lemons, scrubbed and chopped finely, including peel, and avoiding seeds

250 g (9 oz) brown onions, finely diced

2 tablespoons salt

400 g (14 oz) sugar

2 tablespoons brown mustard seeds

1 teaspoon ground ginger

1 teaspoon cayenne pepper

100 g (3½ oz) sultanas (golden raisins)

500 ml (17 fl oz/2 cups) apple cider vinegar

# PICKLED CHERRIES WITH ALLSPICE

**MAKES 1 KG (2 LB 4 OZ)**

Give me a cheese board, a good roast duck, some rillettes and (while very happy, like a Fat Pig in mud) I'm in need of something else to balance the richness. Where we live, we have a surfeit of cherries, and in the season it's worth getting some of the seconds and pickling them for use all year.

*Wash and sterilise four 500 ml (17 fl oz/2 cup) jars (see page 10).*

Check over the cherries well and remove the stalks. Give them a quick rinse to remove any grit.

Bring the vinegar, wine, water, sugar, salt, spices and bay leaf to the boil in a large saucepan or stockpot over searing heat. Turn down the heat and simmer for about 10 minutes to let the flavours infuse. Place the cherries in the jars and warm the bases in warm water. Tip the hot pickling solution over, seal with the lids straightaway, and store in a cool, dark place for 1 month prior to using. Refrigerate once opened.

1 kg (2 lb 4 oz) fresh cherries

600 ml (21 fl oz) red or white wine vinegar

200 ml (7 fl oz) red wine

300 ml (10½ fl oz) water

200 g (7 oz) caster (superfine) sugar

1 teaspoon salt

1 cinnamon stick

1 tablespoon allspice seeds, bruised lightly with the side of a knife

1 teaspoon whole black peppercorns

1 fresh bay leaf

# ALICE MAE'S DILL PICKLES

**MAKES 1.5 KG (3 LB 5 OZ)**

1.5 kg (3 lb 5 oz) small pickling cucumbers, scrubbed

8–10 garlic cloves

a large handful fresh dill (alternatively, use dill flowers or seeds depending on what is available, or dried dill seeds if there is no fresh dill)

2 litres (70 fl oz/8 cups) cold rainwater or filtered water

1 litre (35 fl oz/4 cups) white wine vinegar or quality apple cider vinegar (5% acidity)

150 g (5½ oz) salt

alum powder (available from chemists: ask for food grade)

This is an old American recipe for pickles. It comes from the mother of my former neighbour Duane Moeller. Alice Mae Halferty Moeller had a selection of recipes she handed down to her son. The recipe is actually known in her notes as 'Louise's Dills', named after Alice's grandad's girlfriend, if you can follow the trail. Like all recipes, the important thing to note is that it's very good to hand a good recipe down. Duane and his wife, Joan, recommend Wisconsin picklers and other small specialist varieties. Joan harvests them small, and in the morning, to be pickled whole. If some cukes get away from you and get too big then they can be pickled as spears (quartered or cut into sixths).

If you do grow your own cucumbers, make up extra brine, and store it in the fridge ready to pickle more cukes as they ripen. The alum keeps the pickles crisper, but can be omitted.

*Wash and sterilise eight 500 ml (17 fl oz/2 cup) jars (see page 10).*

Prick cucumbers about 8 times each with a needle or skewer. Peel the garlic and slice in half if cloves are large. Divide the garlic and dill evenly among the jars and pack the cucumbers in tightly.

Make a brine by mixing the water, vinegar and salt, heating if necessary to get the salt to dissolve. Tip this brine over the cucumbers in the jars to cover and add a pinch of alum to each one.

Seal the jars, ideally marking the date on top. Turn upside down for 24 hours, keeping them in the fridge. In 10 days they are ready to eat. They keep well in the fridge for 1 year.

# MUSTARD FRUITS
## (*mostarda di frutta*)

**MAKES 1 KG (2 LB 4 OZ)**

There's something quite delightful about the spicy, sweet, candied fruit of northern Italy. Mustard fruits make a perfect accompaniment to rich sausages, to chicken, even to corned beef. But be warned! This recipe takes four days to prepare.

*Wash and sterilise four 500 ml (17 fl oz/2 cup) jars (see page 10).*

**DAY 1** Cut the fruit into halves or quarters, and it's best if they're all roughly the same size and can fit easily into a jar. Place the fruit in a large nonreactive (glass, ceramic or plastic) bowl and cover with the sugar and the orange juice and zest. Mix well, cover with a tea towel (dish towel) and allow to sit at room temperature for 24 hours.

**DAY 2** The next day, strain all the liquid into a saucepan and bring to the boil, then reduce the heat and simmer for about 5 minutes. Add the fruit, bring back to the boil then quickly remove from heat, pour the mixture back into the bowl and cover again. Stand for another 24 hours.

**DAY 3** Repeat this process the following day, and let it sit for another 24 hours.

**DAY 4** To finish the mostarda, strain the syrup into a saucepan and bring to the boil, then reduce the heat and simmer for 10 minutes. Add the fruits, simmer for 5 more minutes, and then stir in the mustard oil and the vinegar. Stir well and test for flavour. The mustard flavour will mellow a little, so add a little extra as you see fit.

Pour the fruit mixture into sterilised jars, pop on the lids straightaway, allow to cool and then store in the fridge.

1 kg (2 lb 4 oz) mixed fruit (we used figs, cumquats, green cherry tomatoes and crabapples; you could use firm peaches, grapes, apples, apricots or any fruit that's in season really, or try a single variety such as figs)

500 g (1 lb 2 oz) sugar

juice and zest of 1 orange

60–80 ml (2–2½ fl oz/¼–⅓ cup) pungent mustard oil (Italians use a really concentrated mustard essence which is very hard to buy outside of Italy)

2–3 tablespoons apple cider vinegar

*Wholegrain Apple Cider Mustard*
recipe page 127

*Horseradish Mustard*
recipe page 126

# FRENCH-STYLE MUSTARD

MAKES ABOUT 1 KG (2 LB 4 OZ)

One of the defining features of that mouthwatering mustard that the French have mastered is the generous use of verjuice: it's the unfermented juice of unripe grapes, so it's sour, but with a different acid to vinegar. Verjuice adds depth, some sweetness and a lovely mellow flavour. In a pinch you could use lemon juice in its place, from a couple of lemons diluted in 300 ml (10½ fl oz) water. You still want your reduction at the end to be about 600 ml (21 fl oz), so measure as you go.

*Wash and sterilise three 350 ml (12 fl oz) jars (see page 10).*

In a bowl, stir together the mustard flour and 150 ml (5 fl oz) of the verjuice to make a paste.

In a large saucepan, combine the remaining verjuice, the vinegar, French shallots, garlic, bay leaves, peppercorns and cloves. Bring to a simmer over medium heat. Simmer the mixture until reduced to just a third of its original volume. This mix, by the way, will catch your eyes and throat, so use an extraction fan. Strain, discarding the solids, and leave to cool.

Stir the cooled vinegar reduction into the mustard paste. Add the salt, sugar and allspice and stir to combine. Let the mixture stand for at least 20 minutes before transferring to a clean saucepan. Cook for 15 minutes on a low simmer (again, keep your nose and eyes as far away as you practically can, and use an extraction fan: the fumes are notoriously spicy at this stage). Remove from the heat and cool slightly before spooning carefully into sterilised jars and sealing with lids. Leave this mixture at least 1 month before using, as it really is a bit unbalanced and cranky when first made.

The mustard will store for up to 1 year in a cool place. Once opened, store the mustard in the fridge.

500 g (1 lb 2 oz) yellow mustard flour (ground mustard seeds)

1 litre (35 fl oz/4 cups) verjuice

1 litre (35 fl oz/4 cups) white wine vinegar

200 g (7 oz) French shallots, peeled and sliced

5 garlic cloves, crushed

3 fresh bay leaves

20 whole black peppercorns

2 whole cloves

50 g (1¾ oz) salt

50 g (1¾ oz) sugar

½ teaspoon ground allspice

## ⤙ HORSERADISH ⤚ MUSTARD

*To make a rocking horseradish mustard, make the French-style mustard above, then add about 1 tablespoon freshly grated horseradish, or a high quality store-bought horseradish paste, to each cup of ready-to-eat mustard. It's better if left for a day or longer after mixing, or add the horseradish just before bottling if you like.*

# WHOLEGRAIN APPLE CIDER MUSTARD

**MAKES ABOUT 600 G (1 LB 5 OZ)**

150 g (5½ oz) yellow mustard seeds

50 g (1¾ oz) brown mustard seeds

1½ teaspoons ground turmeric

330 ml (11¼ fl oz/1⅓ cups) apple cider

100 ml (3½ fl oz) apple cider vinegar

4 garlic cloves, peeled

1 cinnamon stick

1–2 tablespoons honey

A pungent cider mustard, redolent a little of apples and with a hint of spice, is the perfect accompaniment to our smoky ham. It'll go tremendously with a bacon sandwich, a roast rib eye of beef, some cheese on toast, or anything else you like mustard with, too.

*Wash and sterilise two 300 ml (10⅖ fl oz) jars (see page 10).*

Soak all of the mustard seeds in 250 ml (9 fl oz/1 cup) of water overnight so they soften substantially. Plonk them in a food processor with their soaking juices (most will have been absorbed) and add the turmeric, then blitz well to make a rough paste. Most of the seeds won't break down so it will never be a smooth mustard, but the more you pulse and grind, the pastier it will become. Add a little of the cider as you go if it is too dry to blend. You can use a mortar for part of the mustard if you like to really grind down the seeds.

Heat the remaining apple cider with the vinegar, garlic and cinnamon and boil down to about half the volume. Scoop out the garlic and the cinnamon and add enough of the liquid to the mustard so that it reaches a thick consistency. Stir in the honey, to taste, transfer to sterile jars and store in a cool, dark place such as a pantry for at least a month before using. Once opened, store the mustard in the fridge.

# CHAPTER FIVE:

## Sauces

**E**ggs. Fried and served with little more than potato or rice. A piece of fish. Mushrooms. Steak. They're all quite fine, thank you very much, on their own. But all of them are better with sauce. Not your mass-produced sauce, which is usually just a lot of sugar and maybe tomato concentrate masquerading as flavour. No, real sauce is what we're talking about, where the true alchemy of cooking has turned quite ordinary ingredients into a sublime concoction. We love opening the pantry to reveal shelves groaning with bottles filled with sauce of our own making, just waiting for the opportunity to shine.

Each sauce is a reflection on its origins, a statement about ingredients, and about the magic of cooking. Captured within each one is history, seasonality and above all else, culinary diversity, just waiting for us to tip it on the plate, or use it in a dish.

Mushroom ketchup is the essence of mushrooms, stored for later use. Your sauce of choice could be the chilli garlic version, ready to lift fried rice or a roast chook. A good sauce is all the best flavours, conveniently packaged in a bottle. Whether it's something you use to embellish a dish as you cook it, or after it's cooked, homemade sauce is definitely a cupboard essential.

# REAL BROWN SAUCE

**MAKES ABOUT 2 LITRES (70 FL OZ/8 CUPS)**

Brown sauce is a wonderful concoction, useful on
a bacon sandwich, on bangers; in fact, any time you
need sauce that is a bit spicier than your usual tomato
version. We make ours using apples and plums, and
the result is sublime (in that daggy, 'I'm wearing ugg
boots at 11 am' kind of way).

*Wash and sterilise six or seven 300 ml (10½ fl oz) bottles
(see page 10).*

Put all of the ingredients in a large saucepan and slowly
bring to the boil, stirring occasionally. Reduce the heat to low,
then simmer for about 2 hours, giving it a good stir every now
and then, until thick and syrupy. Push through a food mill
to make a smooth sauce (a food processor works okay, but
a food mill, or mouli, really does make for a better texture).

Return to the pan, then add extra water to achieve a sauce
consistency. It should be pourable, but not thin. Bring back to
the boil, then pour into warmed bottles. Store in a cool, dark
place, and leave it for at least 6 weeks to mellow before using,
though it'll be fine—if not slightly better—after 2 years, too.
Once open, it keeps best in the fridge.

1 kg (2 lb 4 oz) apples, peeled,
cored and chopped

500 g (1 lb 2 oz) plums,
quartered, stones removed

375 g (13 oz) tamarind pulp,
stones removed

1 tablespoon ground ginger

½ teaspoon freshly grated nutmeg

1 teaspoon ground allspice

½ teaspoon cayenne pepper

½ teaspoon ground cloves

100 ml (3½ fl oz) molasses

600 ml (21 fl oz) apple cider
vinegar

500 g (1 lb 2 oz/2⅔ cups lightly
packed) brown sugar

2 tablespoons salt

# NEWLANDS SAUCE
## (Sadie's great-grandma's tomato sauce)

**MAKES ABOUT 10 LITRES (350 FL OZ)**

My partner Sadie's family comes from a property called Newlands in western Victoria. Annie Macmeikan, her great-grandma, passed this recipe down through the family, and it's now been handed on to us at Fat Pig Farm. This is the sauce we call ours, though it does vary slightly from year to year. You want to make a big batch so you've enough to get through the year, and have a bit left over for gifts.

Use your taste as a guide and add spices accordingly. I suspect some modern spices are fresher than they had in the old days, and we use less than the recipe, most of the time. For historical accuracy, however, I've included the original quantities (lest I upset the in-laws ...).

*Wash and sterilise enough bottles and jars for 10 litres (350 fl oz) of sauce (see page 10).*

Peel and core the apples. Wrap the peel and cores in muslin (cheesecloth) and tie with kitchen string to enclose. Chop the apple flesh. Put both the chopped apples and the muslin bag in a big stockpot with the tomato, onion, garlic, salt and vinegar. Bring to a simmer, stirring often so it doesn't stick, and add half of each of the spices, so it doesn't get too spicy. We tend to vary the amount of cloves especially, and add more at the end of all the spices if need be. Simmer for about 2 hours, until the sauce is well cooked and starting to thicken.

1.5 kg (3 lb 5 oz) apples

10 kg (22 lb 8 oz) tomatoes, roughly chopped

1 kg (2 lb 4 oz) brown onions, peeled and chopped

1 garlic bulb, peeled

220 g (7¾ oz) salt

1.5 litres (52 fl oz/6 cups) white or malt vinegar

30 g (1 oz) ground ginger

30 g (1 oz) ground mace

15 g (½ oz) cayenne pepper

60 g (2 oz) ground allspice

60 g (2 oz) ground cloves

2 kg (4 lb 8 oz) sugar, to taste

Remove and discard the bag of apple cores. Using a stick blender, blend the sauce well, return to the stove in a clean pan, and cook down until the correct consistency (which is thick enough to sit on a pork sausage, but not so thick that it doesn't come out of the bottle!).

Add three-quarters of the sugar, stir well and taste. It should be quite strong in terms of being sweet/sour/salty, compared to a soup or a stew. Remember, you only use a small amount each time you use it and the flavour needs to reflect that. Adjust the seasoning and spices as you see fit.

When ready, pour into the prepared bottles or jars. (Remember, the glass will crack if it changes temperature too rapidly, so hot liquid should go into prewarmed jars.) Seal the bottles and it should keep well for at least a year, if not 2 or 3 years.

**NOTE:** *The amount of sugar and vinegar can vary because of the variation in tomatoes. I've decided to keep the vinegar constant and just adjust the sugar, this way making sure the sauce doesn't go off, as the acid acts as a strong preservative.*

*Newlands Sauce*
recipe page 134

*Tomato Passata*
recipe page 138

# TOMATO PASSATA

**MAKES ABOUT 12 LITRES (420 FL OZ)**

Passata is just a fresh tomato purée. Traditionally, passata is made right at the end of summer or in autumn, when there's a glut of ripe, juicy tomatoes, and it's put into bottles so you don't have to use electricity to keep it frozen all year. You pull out a bottle midwinter and get a flash of summer warmth in any recipe you cook.

*Wash and sterilise enough beer bottles or wide-mouthed bottles for 12 litres (420 fl oz) of passata (see page 10).*

Heat a big stockpot of water to a simmer for blanching. Simply wash good tomatoes and cut out any bad bits. If you have a bruised tomato, that bit might cause your passata to ferment, so it's better to discard it now than ruin the whole batch. Plunge the tomatoes into the simmering water in batches to loosen the skin, which should only take about 15–20 seconds if they're ripe. Scoop them out using a spider or similar slotted spoon and put them in a colander.

Let them cool, a bit. I like to mash the tomatoes up with my hands a little (which helps later on with the milling) and leave them in the colander for a few minutes over a bowl, keeping the free-flowing juice that comes out of the colander in one pot. I then put the flesh through a food mill or, ideally, a proper passata mill which you can find at good kitchen equipment shops. The passata mill separates the skin and seeds from the pulp, unlike a food processor, which mangles

at least 20 kg (45 lb) very ripe tomatoes, ideally roma (plum) tomatoes as they have the best yield

*We try to make passata days a celebration: a day of family, of fun, all the while preserving the taste of summer for all seasons.*

them all up and delivers a coarser flavoured sauce. If you're doing a lot of tomatoes, there's an attachment you can get for your mincer that works so fast and effectively you'll never want to do it by hand again. I put each batch through twice to extract all the pulp.

The thin liquid I use for soup that same day or soon after; the thicker liquid, which includes the tomato pulp, I store as my passata.

Bottle the passata in beer bottles or, even better, in wide-mouthed bottles (the passata can be a bit textured, which is ideal). Some people add a basil leaf or a chilli to each jar at this stage, but I tend to leave my passata very pure and add flavours when I open the bottles later. Top the bottles with sterilised caps, and stand them in a large stockpot, lined with tea towels (dish towels) to prevent the jars cracking as they jostle. Fill the pot with water so that the bottles are completely submerged, heat over high heat until the water boils, then simmer for a couple of hours to pasteurise and preserve the passata. Take care when removing the jars (or leave them to cool in the water), and store them in a cool, dark place. (See page 10 for more details about pasteurising.)

I've kept passata for up to 2½ years without losing its quality.

# AMERICAN-STYLE BARBECUE SAUCE

**MAKES ENOUGH TO RUB ON ABOUT SIX WHOLE PORK RIB RACKS**

This is Sadie's family recipe for an American-style barbecue sauce, which is used as a marinade rather than as a sauce to put on at the end. Don't be scared by the list of ingredients, as most are commonplace: if you make a double batch, it freezes well for later use or can be stored in sterilised bottles. I love it on pork spare ribs, marinated overnight, then roasted over low heat on a smoky barbecue or chargrill, or on beef brisket, cooked long and slow on a covered barbecue.

*Wash and sterilise two 300 ml (10½ fl oz) jars (see page 10).*

Heat the olive oil in a large, heavy-based frying pan over low heat and fry the onion for 5 minutes or until soft. Add the ginger, cumin, coriander, paprika and chilli and keep frying gently for about 5 minutes until fragrant. Don't let the spices brown and burn.

Add the other ingredients and simmer gently for 15 minutes, stirring occasionally and checking that the pan doesn't dry out (add a tablespoon of water if it's looking dry). Transfer to sterile jars, then boil the jars to pasteurise them (see page 10). It keeps well for up to a year.

When using the marinade, it's best to marinate the meat in it first and cook over very low heat, with some moisture, adding more marinade as it cooks. The outsides will go dark: just take care it doesn't actually burn as the sugars in the sauce can taste a bit acrid if actually burnt (though, remember, the insides will taste great anyway if that does happen).

1 tablespoon olive oil

½ small red (Spanish) onion, finely diced

1 teaspoon freshly grated ginger

½ teaspoon cumin seeds

1 teaspoon ground coriander

1 tablespoon sweet paprika

1–2 teaspoons chilli powder

½ lemon, seeds removed, chopped finely

2 tablespoons cider or white wine vinegar

60 ml (2 fl oz/¼ cup) lemon juice

2 tablespoons brown sugar

1 teaspoon mustard powder

400 g (14 oz) tin crushed Italian tomatoes

1 tablespoon Worcestershire Sauce (see page 142, or use a ready-made version)

1 teaspoon salt

½ teaspoon freshly ground black pepper

# AUSTRALIAN-STYLE BARBECUE SAUCE

**MAKES ABOUT 500 ML (17 FL OZ/2 CUPS)**

500 ml (17 fl oz/2 cups) Newlands
Sauce (see page 134, or use a
good ready-made tomato sauce)

2 tablespoons Mushroom Ketchup
(see page 145), if you have it

1 teaspoon smoked paprika

2 tablespoons Worcestershire
Sauce (see page 142, or use
a ready-made version)

1 tablespoon treacle (or molasses)

1 teaspoon finely grated lemon zest

1 tablespoon lemon juice

This barbecue sauce is a variation on tomato sauce, which is popular in Australia. I like to add smokiness (which is reminiscent of the barbecue) through the use of smoked paprika, a slight bitter sweetness from treacle, and the complexity of Worcestershire sauce to round it out. A good barbecue sauce goes amazingly well on a steak sandwich with nothing more than white bread and some browned sliced onions.

*Wash and sterilise a 500 ml (17 fl oz/2 cup) bottle or two smaller bottles (see page 10).*

Heat all of the ingredients together in a large saucepan over high heat, adding about 100 ml (3½ fl oz) of water. When it comes to the boil, turn down to a simmer and cook for about 30 minutes until thickened, stirring occasionally. Transfer to the sterile bottle, seal and store for about a month prior to using for best results. You can use it straightaway, too. Once opened, store it in the fridge and use within a month or two.

# WORCESTERSHIRE SAUCE

MAKES ABOUT 2.5 LITRES (87 FL OZ/10 CUPS)

Some might say it's not Worcestershire sauce unless it's come from Worcestershire. Well, that may be true, but what else should we call our version of this classic dark sauce? Some say never to shake the bottle, lest you upset its contents. Some say never to open the bottle until it's been in the cellar for a year (we do think that's a good thing, too). Others may say it's not the real deal unless it has the requisite anchovies in it. But we say regardless of anything else, it's a must-have in the pantry, and this is a cracking version you can whip up easily at home.

*Wash and sterilise eight or nine 300 ml (10½ fl oz) bottles (see page 10).*

Roughly chop and core the apples, garlic and onion and put them in a large saucepan. Add enough water to cover and bring to the boil. Cook to a pulp: about an hour or so, to really soften the onion. Press through a fine-meshed sieve, or through a mouli (food mill), into a bowl. Wash out the saucepan and return the strained paste to the pan with any remaining water in the pot.

Add the salt, vinegar, spices, chillies, tamarind and sugar, stirring over medium heat until the sugar has dissolved. Increase the heat to high and keep on a rolling boil for 3 hours. Add the treacle and boil for another 30 minutes. Strain and pour into sterilised bottles. You might think it tastes awful and this is a rubbish recipe. But trust me, allow it to mellow for at least 3 weeks (preferably longer) and you'll be calling yourself Lea & Perrins. This sauce keeps for years and is, in fact, better after a year forgotten in the back of the pantry. Once it's open, however, store it in the fridge to keep the flavour fresh.

1 kg (2 lb 4 oz) apples (also works with plums or a combination of both)

2 garlic cloves, peeled

1 onion, peeled

250 g (9 oz) salt

4 litres (140 fl oz/16 cups) apple cider vinegar

2 teaspoons ground allspice

100 g (3½ oz) whole black peppercorns

½ teaspoon ground cloves

2 red chillies, coarsely chopped

1 tablespoon tamarind pulp

80 g (2¾ oz) sugar

350 g (12 oz/1 cup) treacle (or molasses)

# NUN'S SAUCE
## (a spicy garlic anchovy sauce)

**MAKES ABOUT 750 ML (26 FL OZ/3 CUPS)**

This recipe, inspired by Dorothy Hartley's version in *Food in England*, is a heady mix of things that go well together. In Dorothy's version, you leave it at the bottom of the stairs so that everybody who goes past (on their way to chapel, because the nuns were the ones making it) gives it a jiggle to keep it well stirred up. You can do it at home and just try to remember to swizzle it around every day or so while it steeps.

*Wash and sterilise a 750 ml (26 fl oz/3 cup) jar or equivalent (see page 10).*

Put all of the ingredients in a nonreactive container (glass, plastic or ceramic). I find a big jar works really well. Cover and leave in a cool place (ideally not a fridge) for a month, giving it a jiggle or shake every day to help it do its thing.

After a month, taste it. It should be hot and sharp and salty and interesting. If it needs longer, leave it longer. If you think it's ready, strain and put the liquid in a sterile bottle in the fridge. Keeps well for several months, though it's best in the first month after you decant it.

4 anchovies (ideally salted, but in oil is fine), roughly chopped

3 very hot chillies, or to taste, coarsely chopped

250 ml (9 fl oz/1 cup) soy sauce

4 garlic cloves, peeled and crushed with a knife

3–4 French shallots, peeled and sliced

500 ml (17 fl oz/2 cups) white wine vinegar

1 tablespoon sugar

# MUSHROOM KETCHUP

**MAKES ABOUT 750 ML (26 FL OZ/3 CUPS)**

1 kg (2 lb 4 oz) field mushrooms

4 French shallots, peeled and
  thinly sliced

50 g (1¾ oz) salt

3 mace blades

2 whole cloves

1 tablespoon whole black
  peppercorns

1 fresh bay leaf

500 ml (17 fl oz/2 cups) malt
  vinegar

2½ tablespoons brandy

This is a wonderful use of big flat mushrooms, especially the horse mushrooms that sometimes bob up in our paddocks. You can use bought 'field' or flat mushrooms, though it's worth waiting until they're on special and doing a big batch to save a few coins. The result is an earthy intense sauce that's quite sharp from the vinegar, but adds great depth to other sauces, gravies, or is quite magic tipped over sliced onions that have come straight from the barbecue.

*Wash and sterilise a 750 ml (26 fl oz/3 cup) bottle or equivalent (see page 10).*

Slice the mushrooms thinly, pop them into a big nonreactive bowl (glass, plastic or ceramic) with the French shallots, sprinkle with the salt, toss well and leave overnight in a cool place. The salt will have drawn out the moisture and the mushrooms will have become soft.

Preheat the oven to 150°C (300°F). Mangle the mushrooms up well by smashing them with a wooden spoon or similar. Put them in a baking dish with their soaking juices, the spices, bay leaf and vinegar and cook for about 1½ hours. Remove from the oven and strain the mushrooms, pressing well to extract as much juice as possible. Add the brandy, stir through and pour the sauce into a sterilised bottle. Put on the lid and then stand the bottle on a tea towel (dish towel) in a preserving kettle or similar deep saucepan. Cover with water, bring to the boil and simmer for an hour. This pasteurises the ketchup and helps to stop it going off. (See page 10 for more details about pasteurisation.)

Mushroom ketchup will keep really well, unopened, for years if pasteurised properly, gaining more attraction as it ages. Once opened, keep it in the fridge and use within a month.

# SAMBAL OELEK CHILLI PASTE

**MAKES 170 G (6 OZ)**

Sambal oelek, oftened shortened to sambal, is an Indonesian chilli paste. At its heart it's simply crushed or ground chillies (ideally using a mortar and pestle) with a little vinegar and salt. It's dead easy to make. What's better, no waiting!

*Wash and sterilise a small jar (see page 10) if you don't plan to use this within a day or two of making.*

Remove the stems from the chillies and chop roughly. Grind using a mortar and pestle, or pulse in a small food processor if that's all you have, until it's finely ground, adding the salt as it goes.

Add the vinegar, a little at a time if you're using a food processor, to add moisture which can help the mixture blend. I find the quantity of vinegar needed varies a bit, so add the last 2 teaspoons at the end.

The sambal is ready to eat straightaway, though I think it's better a day later, or it can be stored in a sterile jar in the fridge for several weeks.

125 g (4½ oz) red chillies, heat depending on your tolerance, but the sauce is supposed to be hot

1 teaspoon salt, or to taste

1½–2 tablespoons distilled white vinegar (tamarind makes a nice option)

# SRIRACHA CHILLI PASTE

**MAKES 200 G (7 OZ)**

125 g (4½ oz) red chillies, ideally
    hot ones or a mix

1 teaspoon salt, or to taste

finely grated zest and juice of
    1 lime

1 teaspoon freshly grated ginger

1 small garlic clove, grated

1 tablespoon grated palm sugar
    (jaggery)

1–2 tablespoons distilled white
    vinegar (ideally rice vinegar)

If you prefer a little more complexity of flavour, the sweetness often favoured by the Thais is evident in sriracha, which has a looser consistency than its sister sambal oelek (see opposite).

*Wash and sterilise a small jar (see page 10).*

Remove the stems from the chillies and chop roughly. Grind using a mortar and pestle, or pulse in a small food processor if that's all you have, until it's finely ground, adding the salt, lime zest, ginger and garlic as you go. When it's a fine paste, add the palm sugar, lime juice and vinegar. Taste, as you may want a touch more sugar depending on your palate.

Store in a sterile jar in the fridge for at least 2 weeks before using, and it's then best used within a month or two.

# CHILLI GARLIC SAUCE

**MAKES ABOUT 2.25 LITRES (79 FL OZ/9 CUPS)**

350 ml (12 fl oz) olive oil

250 g (9 oz) large red chillies, roughly chopped

2 kg (4 lb 8 oz) tomatoes, roughly chopped

30 garlic cloves, crushed

150 g (5½ oz) sugar

large knob of fresh ginger, bashed

350 ml (12 fl oz) apple cider vinegar

2 tablespoons hot smoked paprika

2 tablespoons yellow mustard seeds

1½ tablespoons ground turmeric

4 tablespoons ground cumin

1 tablespoon salt

This wonderful sauce could also be used as a relish if you make it just a bit thicker. Almost as popular as the Fat Pig Buns we serve at festivals, and with SO many people clamouring for the recipe, it's the least we could do to include it here.

*Wash and sterilise three 750 ml (26 fl oz/3 cup) bottles (see page 10).*

Heat the olive oil in a large saucepan over low heat and add the chilli, tomato and garlic. Cook slowly for a few minutes until the chilli and garlic soften and the tomato surrenders its juices. Add all of the remaining ingredients and simmer over very low heat for at least 3 hours until thickened. Give it a good stir every now and then, scraping any caramelised bits that stick to the side of the saucepan back into the sauce. The sauce often shows that it's ready when the oil floats to the surface. Remove from the heat, then use a stick blender to purée it until completely smooth.

Pour the still warm sauce into sterile bottles and seal. Store in a cool, dry and dark place for at least 2 weeks to allow the flavours to develop before eating. Then pour into squeezy bottles to serve at your next event!

# EAST TIMORESE INSPIRED FERMENTED CHILLI SAUCE

**MAKES ABOUT 600 ML (21 FL OZ)**

This recipe takes the wonderful flavour of chillies and makes them more complex through a process of fermentation. Fermentation is actually one way in which food decays or rots, so there's always the chance it may go a little awry. Mould may grow on top and take over the chilli, it could ferment a little too fast or too slow, but generally it's really a simple way to create an amazing chilli sauce. This is my attempt to recreate the sauce I fell in love with when I went to East Timor in the early 2000s.

about 500 g (1 lb 2 oz) red chillies

3–4 garlic cloves

2–3 tablespoons salt

500 ml (17 fl oz/2 cups) white vinegar (ideally from rice or similar)

1 basil sprig

Blend the chillies in a food processor with the garlic until they form a fine paste (seeds are fine left whole) and place in a nonreactive bowl (glass, plastic or ceramic) or crock. Ideally, you want the crock to be deeper with a smaller top, rather than too small. If you only have a big container, make more sauce, as the top of the chillies tends to oxidise and is discarded. I find a jar is the best solution. Sprinkle the top with salt, ideally about 2 tablespoons, to create a layer that will dissolve quite quickly. Cover with a cloth (a lid won't let the chilli breathe, which they need to do to ferment). The next day, check that there's a layer of liquid on top, drawn out by the salt. If not, add a little more salt where needed to draw out the moisture. Next day check again, and top with a tiny bit of water if need be.

*The best sauces in the pantry are the most complicated in flavour. Some achieve it with a long list of ingredients; some through fermentation; and almost all by virtue of their age.*

This mixture needs to stand for about a month, in a cool place (12°C/54°F), ideally in the dark and away from the breeze. A cellar is excellent, a pantry is okay. The mixture will start to become more fragrant as the chillies ferment, not always in an attractive way. Check the top for mould and add a tiny sprinkle of salt to the top if it's getting a bit too mouldy.

After about 4 weeks, taking care not to tip the jar too much, spoon off any mould on the top. It is likely it will have gone a little festy (a white scum is usual). Use paper towel to clean any mould off the crock or jar, then tip the fermented paste into a big bowl. Add the vinegar and the basil, then cover with a cloth and leave this mixture to stand, at room temperature, for another week at least, ideally two.

Strain the sauce through a colander (some chunks make it more attractive, hence a colander, not a sieve), and transfer it to sterilised jars (see page 10). It's ready to use straightaway, though I prefer it a month later.

Some add a little sugar to it now, or even a bit of coriander root. Use on chicken, in stir-fries, with rice, or any place you want an interesting chilli sauce.

# MINT SAUCE

**MAKES JUST UNDER 300 ML (10½ FL OZ)**

250 ml (9 fl oz/1 cup) malt vinegar

1 teaspoon soy sauce

1 teaspoon sugar

3 tablespoons finely chopped
mint leaves

The must-have accompaniment to roast lamb is a very easy sauce to make, and it gets better with a little time in the pantry. We like the addition of a waft of soy sauce to add even more charm to the original. There's also a Mint Jelly (on page 71) if that's more your thing, though it is more work to prepare.

*Wash and sterilise one 300 ml (10½ fl oz) jar (see page 10).*

Put the malt vinegar, soy sauce and sugar in a decent-size bowl and whisk to dissolve the sugar. Add the mint and decant to the prepared jar. You can use it immediately, but it's a bit better if you seal it and leave it in the pantry for a month before using.

# CHAPTER SIX:

# Curds + Butters

A good curd, sometimes called a butter, is a fine thing to have made. I feel warm and fuzzy putting up a few jars of curd in the season when the chooks are laying and the time permits. Most often, I make a kilogram of curd, knowing we can't eat it all. That way a jar or two will be given to friends, in the secret hope that they may reciprocate one day. Often they do, but with a different curd, or a bottle of preserved fruit, or an invitation to tea.

Real homemade citrus curds (and apple butter) don't resemble the commercial varieties that—I think, shamefully—share their name. The homemade versions are simple spreads that have so many other uses beyond breakfast toast. That's why I've put a basic lemon curd in at least two of my other recipe books. I use curd for dessert with meringue, in trifles, even in or with ice cream. You can spread a curd on the base of tarts, use it in a fool, use it with puff pastry or in a croissant.

Most of all, a curd will find a use. Once you go to the small amount of effort to put some in the fridge, that is.

# PASSIONFRUIT CURD

**MAKES NEARLY THREE CUPS—750 G (1 LB 10 OZ)**

If the passionfruit are a bit dry, push the flesh through a sieve so you don't end up with too many seeds, and only return half the seeds to the curd.

*Wash and sterilise three 250 ml (9 fl oz/1 cup) jars (see page 10).*

In the top of a double boiler, or a heatproof bowl over a saucepan of simmering water, melt all the ingredients together, stirring occasionally with a wooden spoon. Once melted, keep stirring over simmering water until thickened slightly, being sure to run your spoon over the bottom as you stir. The base of the bowl is obviously the hottest point, so you want to even out the heat and the cooking by stirring it evenly and well. It will take about 10 minutes, but could be as little as 5 or as long as 15 before it thickens.

It also thickens more as it cools. Transfer to sterile jars and store in the fridge for a month at the outside.

250 g (9 oz/1 cup) passionfruit pulp (about 10–12 passionfruit), whisked to create an even consistency

finely grated zest and strained juice of 1 lemon

4 eggs, lightly beaten

150 g (5½ oz) unsalted butter

200 g (7 oz) caster (superfine) sugar

# APPLE BUTTER WITH LEATHERWOOD HONEY & CINNAMON

**MAKES ABOUT 1 KG (2 LB 4 OZ)**

2 kg (4 lb 8 oz) tart apples, such as golden delicious, cox's orange pippin or similar

2 cinnamon sticks

1 kg (2 lb 4 oz) brown sugar

about 3 tablespoons leatherwood honey

There are several ways to make this delightful sweet concoction. Some don't use sugar, some actually add butter. This version reduces apple and sugar, then scents it with leatherwood honey. It's a terrific spread for toast but is equally at home in the base of fruit tarts or with pancakes.

*Wash and sterilise four 250 ml (9 fl oz/1 cup) jars (see page 10).*

Chop the apples, including the peel and cores. Toss them into a large saucepan and just cover with water. Add the cinnamon sticks and simmer over medium heat until the apples are really soft.

Remove the cinnamon sticks and put the apple and any liquid through a food mill. A food processor simply won't work, because it crushes the seeds. You could push it through a sieve if you've more patience than me.

Put the apple purée into a clean saucepan—ideally a jam pan or similar (see page 15)—with the sugar and put the heat on low. Stir over this low heat until the sugar is dissolved. Reduce heat to a mere murmur, and simmer for about 2 hours until dark, thick and jammy, stirring often to prevent the apple catching. When it's thick and pasty, add the honey, adding more to taste if you think it needs it. Pour the butter into the sterile jars and seal. You can store this in a cool pantry, but it's best kept in the fridge.

# MANDARIN
# & LEMON CURD

**MAKES ABOUT 1 KG (2 LB 4 OZ)**

This is a lovely, fragrant use for mandarins in season. If the fruit is difficult to zest, put it in the freezer for 30 minutes to firm up. Sterilise the jars before you start cooking the curd.

*Wash and sterilise four 250 ml (9 fl oz/1 cup) jars (see page 10).*

Grate the citrus peel using a fine-toothed grater. Juice and remove all the seeds (you can strain it, but I don't).

Combine all of the ingredients in a heatproof bowl over a saucepan of simmering water or in the top of a double boiler and stir gently until the butter melts. Continue cooking, stirring to scrape the bottom constantly, for 5 minutes or until the curd thickens nicely. If it goes a bit lumpy you can whisk it, but don't cook it too long or it will scramble and separate. Cool a little and transfer to the sterile jars and seal.

Store in the fridge for up to 1 month and use on toast, fruit bread or in tarts.

| 4 lemons |
| --- |
| 2 honey murcott mandarins, or similar |
| 8 eggs, lightly beaten |
| 200 g (7 oz) butter, diced |
| 400 g (14 oz) caster (superfine) sugar |

# LEMON LIME CURD

**MAKES ABOUT 1 KG (2 LB 4 OZ)**

finely grated zest and strained
  juice of 2 lemons

finely grated zest and strained
  juice of 4 limes

6 eggs, lightly beaten

300 g (10½ oz) unsalted butter

200 g (7 oz) caster (superfine)
  sugar

**This curd is quite tart compared to some that we make, and more buttery. It's a lovely sharp concoction that goes really well in a tart with a sweet shortcrust base and topped with fruit, or simply spooned onto brioche or panettone and gobbled up for Sunday brunch. I recommend making it when the limes are at their lowest price, which isn't in early summer.**

*Wash and sterilise four 250 ml (9 fl oz/1 cup) jars (see page 10).*

Combine all of the ingredients in the top of a double boiler (or in a heatproof bowl over a saucepan of simmering water). Melt the ingredients (except the zest, which won't melt), stirring occasionally with a wooden spoon. Once melted, keep stirring this mixture over simmering water until it starts to thicken, rubbing your spoon or spatula over the bottom as you go. You're probably looking at about 10 minutes but it could take longer or less time.

Transfer to sterile jars, seal and store in the fridge for up to a month.

# MICHELLE'S INSANELY GOOD BLACKCURRANT CURD

**MAKES ABOUT 750 G (1 LB 10 OZ/3 CUPS)**

250 g (9 oz) blackcurrants

130 g (4½ oz) unsalted butter

180 g (6½ oz) caster (superfine) sugar

4 eggs, beaten

Fragrant with blackcurrant and dark to boot, this is a lush, rich curd that our friend/researcher/jam-maker and stylist Michelle Crawford perfected. It resembles its lemony cousin in name, more than flavour. You could use this curd in tarts or on bread, but it is often eaten in large spoonfuls from the jar in our house.

*Wash and sterilise three 250 ml (9 fl oz/1 cup) jars (see page 10).*

Prepare the blackcurrants by putting them in a saucepan with 1 tablespoon of water. Cook over medium heat until the blackcurrant skins have burst and released all the juice. This is important, because you really want as much juice and flavour as possible, but overcooking can tend to make the curd taste a little tired.

Strain the fruit through a fine sieve into a jug and collect the purée, rubbing gently with a plastic spatula. If you press hard, you'll get pulp, which isn't ideal. You'll need 100 ml (3½ fl oz) of blackcurrant purée.

To make the curd, bring a medium saucepan of water to the boil. Put the butter and sugar into a heatproof bowl. Turn the water down to a simmer then set the bowl over the saucepan (make sure the bottom of the bowl doesn't touch the water) and stir until the sugar has dissolved.

Add the eggs to the butter mixture, then add the blackcurrant purée and whisk until well combined. Switch from the whisk to a wooden spoon and stir the mixture constantly until it thickens and coats the back of the spoon; this should take about 20 minutes or even less. (If you have a thermometer, it thickens at about 82°C (180°F), which may make keeping an eye on it a little easier.) Pour through a clean sieve and into the sterilised jars. Store in the fridge for up to 1 month.

# MANDARIN HONEY BUTTER

**MAKES ABOUT 250 G (9 OZ)**

This is a fantastic butter to keep in the fridge for quick pancakes, or to melt into crumpets. The mandarin is pretty lovely, but it can be hard to grate the zest from some mandarins. We use the honey murcott variety, when available, for the easiest zest, or freeze them for half an hour to make the skin firm up.

Grate the zest from the mandarins and juice them. If the skin is impossible to grate, juice them first then remove the peel; run a knife over the peel to remove the white pith and chop about 1 tablespoon of the peel as finely as you can.

Combine the butter with the icing sugar in a food processor until the mixture is pale, light and fluffy. Add the juice, zest and honey and pulse to incorporate. Blend again, scraping down the side, to make a fairly smooth, light butter. You can roll it in foil, refrigerate and slice it into discs when ready, if you're really keen, or just spoon off bits to melt onto pancakes.

The butter must be kept in the fridge when not in use, and will keep for only about 3 weeks or so.

2 firm honey murcott mandarins, or similar

150 g (5½ oz) butter, softened

2 tablespoons icing (confectioners') sugar

3 tablespoons honey or maple syrup

# BRANDY BUTTER
## *(ideal for Christmas)*

**MAKES ABOUT 400 G (14 OZ)**

200 g (7 oz) butter, softened

150 g (5½ oz/⅔ cup) brown sugar

2 tablespoons boiling water

1 teaspoon finely grated lemon zest

80 ml (2½ fl oz/⅓ cup) brandy
   (or try rum, which is pretty
   fantastic, too)

Known as a 'hard sauce' and often served with Christmas pudding, brandy butter is actually a really nice thing to have in the house at other times. I can recommend it grilled onto halved peaches, melted over apples to eat with crepes, or even dripping into homemade crumpets.

Using an electric mixer fitted with the beater attachment, beat the butter with the sugar until pale and light. Beat in the boiling water and lemon zest, then when it's all combined, beat in the brandy, 1 tablespoon at a time.

Store in an airtight container in the fridge. You can make it into rolls (use plastic wrap and twist the ends), which can be sliced later for easier use. The butter will keep for a couple of months in the fridge, but really it's best used within a month.

# CHAPTER SEVEN:

# Cordials, Squashes + Syrups

We're quite the fans of a squash. And a cordial. And a syrup that can be used for all sorts of desserts. Bottled concentrates are a saviour on a hot summer's day, when lemonade goes down a treat with kids and grown-ups alike. Weekend pancakes are always better with a little strawberry syrup. Winter nights warm up nicely thanks to a spicy, gingery hot toddy made with our own ginger ale concentrate. And what's not to like about the anise-scented blackcurrant squash?

When we look in our fridge and find a little rhubarb squash, we think of ways it might lift a fig tart, or a bowl of natural yoghurt, as much as it might make the drink that gives it its name. We see a judicious use of the surplus of the seasons—and the excess from our neighbours' freezers—all kept longer than the fruit from which it came. But most of all, we just adore the look of a shelf of syrups that can turn into more drinks, desserts, brunches and suppers than you care to count.

# APPLE SYRUP

MAKES ABOUT 500 ML (17 FL OZ/2 CUPS) OF CONCENTRATE

Apple syrup is a lovely, condensed version of apple juice. In areas that don't have maple trees, it is sometimes used in the place of maple syrup, because as it boils down you end up with a similar type of syrup that is both sour and sweet. While maple has, perhaps, more nuance, apple syrup more than makes up for that with its delicious flavour and range of uses. We put it on pancakes, on crumpets or over ice cream with a few roasted hazelnuts. We've used it in drinks, to flavour cream for cakes: the list goes on. Ideally, buy apple juice from a local company in bulk to justify the energy used to reduce it down. You can add a whole clove or two or a cinnamon stick to give it another dimension. Cheats may use a little sugar to help speed up the process and give a greater yield, but we think the pure sweetness of the apple is best unadulterated.

*Wash and sterilise a 500 ml (17 fl oz/2 cup) bottle (see page 10).*

Put the apple juice in as wide a pan as you have. (Wider means it will reduce quicker.) Bring it to the boil over high heat, then turn it down to a simmer. You want the apple juice to get to about 10 per cent of its original volume.

Simmer the juice right down, perhaps rubbing a spatula over the bottom of the pan every now and then to ensure it's not catching. The consistency you're looking for is pretty much identical to maple syrup, so test on a saucer that's been chilled in the fridge (as hot sauce is always runny).

When ready, pour into the warmed bottle and store in the pantry until opened, then store in the fridge.

5 litres (175 fl oz/20 cups) cloudy apple juice (pasteurised is fine)

# RASPBERRY &
# PEACH CORDIAL

**MAKES ABOUT 1 LITRE (35 FL OZ/4 CUPS) OF CONCENTRATE**

This flavour combination, reminiscent of the classic peach Melba, makes for a lovely syrup. The end result can be used for breakfast, with dessert, or to make a very attractive coloured, and flavoured, drink.

*Wash and sterilise one 1 litre (35 fl oz/4 cup) or two 500 ml (17 fl oz/2 cup) bottles (see page 10).*

Put the vanilla bean and 1.5 litres (52 fl oz/6 cups) of water in a very large saucepan over high heat. Bring to the boil, then turn down to a simmer for 10 minutes and then remove the vanilla bean (it can be dried and used for vanilla sugar or in custard).

Juice the lemons and reserve both the juice and the peel.

Bring the vanilla water back to the boil, turn off the heat, then immediately add the fruit, including the lemon peel (but not the lemon juice). The water should just cover the fruit: if not, boil the kettle and top it up.

Leave this mixture to stand until cool, about 2 hours at least. Drain the fruit through a sieve into a large bowl (don't press it through the sieve, just let gravity do the work), and whisk in the lemon juice, then whisk the sugar into the liquid to taste. It's a concentrate, so it should be quite sweet and flavoursome, but not cloying. You can keep the steeped peaches for use in a breakfast trifle or similar, though they will have lost some of their wonder to the syrup.

Transfer the syrup to the sterilised bottle(s) and store in the fridge for up to a month before using.

1 vanilla bean, split lengthways

2 lemons

1 kg (2 lb 4 oz) ripe peaches, stones removed, cut into wedges

250 g (9 oz/2 cups) raspberries

about 220 g (7¾ oz/1 cup) caster (superfine) sugar

# GINGER ALE SYRUP

**MAKES ABOUT 400 ML (14 FL OZ) OF CONCENTRATE**

100 g (3½ oz) ginger

4 lemons, scrubbed

2–3 tablespoons honey

3–4 tablespoons raw caster
(superfine) sugar

We make a cracking ginger ale that we serve as a hot toddy in winter and as a refreshing cool drink in summer. We, however, don't grow the ginger; instead leaving that to folk from further north.

*Wash and sterilise a 500 ml (17 fl oz/2 cup) bottle (see page 10).*

Scrub the ginger well, making sure you get between any tight bits so there's no dirt in the end drink. Snap it at the joins if need be. Bruise the ginger with the back of a knife, or slice roughly. Plonk it in a large saucepan with about 500 ml (17 fl oz/2 cups) of water and bring to the boil over lively heat. Reduce the heat and barely simmer for about 1 hour.

Juice the lemons, reserving both the juice and the peel. Add the peel to the pot, topping up with enough water to cover, and bring back to a simmer. Cook like this, ensuring the water level stays above the lemons and weighing them down with a plate if need be, for 30 minutes. You'll probably have to top up with boiling water from the kettle. Turn the heat off and let the ginger and lemon steep in the liquid for at least 1 hour (you can leave it for longer and it's fine) then strain the liquid into a clean saucepan. Heat it slightly, add the honey and sugar and stir to dissolve. Add the strained lemon juice and adjust the flavour with sugar to taste (you may also want to use more honey; it can depend on how floral your honey is). When it tastes … well … gingery and lemony and not too sweet, it's ready.

Transfer the syrup to the sterilised bottle and seal. Store in the fridge for up to 1 month. This is a little concentrated, so you'll need to water it down slightly to drink. In summer we use soda water, in winter we add water, then heat it, and serve it with a nip of Tasmanian whisky or other spirits.

# REAL HOMEMADE LEMONADE

**SERVES 5–6**

5 lemons, well scrubbed

1 litre (35 fl oz/4 cups) water

250 g (9 oz) caster (superfine) sugar

This is a great, simple zesty drink that doesn't resemble fizzy soft drink at all.

Remove the zest from the lemons with a zester, or with a potato peeler, trying to avoid the white pith. If using a potato peeler, lay the zest skin side down on a chopping board, and use a small knife to very carefully scrape off any of the pith and discard. This white pith can make the lemonade a little bitter. That's okay in moderation, but for the kids it's a bit too much. Juice the lemons and reserve the juice, discarding any seeds.

Put the zest in a saucepan with the water and bring to just under a simmer (don't let it boil). Poach gently for 10 minutes, then turn off the heat and allow to steep a further 10 minutes. Strain and whisk in the sugar until it dissolves (reheat if necessary). Cool, add the lemon juice and refrigerate. Serve with ice and a little water for the kids, or with soda water and something stronger as a hair of the dog.

# BLUEBERRY, LEMON & NUTMEG SYRUP

**MAKES ABOUT 1.5 LITRES (52 FL OZ/6 CUPS) OF CONCENTRATE**

You'd never make this if you had to pay big bucks for a tiny punnet of blueberries at the greengrocer. But where we live they grow plenty of them, and you can sometimes pick up seconds quite cheaply. It's then that we look for other uses rather than just gobbling them up fresh. These flavourings go quite well with blackcurrants, too, but they cook differently, so tweak the method and sugar as per page 182.

*Wash and sterilise three 500 ml (17 fl oz/2 cup) bottles (see page 10).*

Put the blueberries, lemon peel, nutmeg and bay leaf in a large saucepan with 1 litre (35 fl oz/4 cups) of water. Bring to the boil, reduce the heat and simmer for about 10 minutes or until the berries are really soft. Set aside to cool in the saucepan; a few hours is best.

Drain the berries through a sieve, pressing gently to extract as much of the flavour and soft pulp, as possible. Discard the solids (or find a dessert that uses slightly watery-flavoured blueberry skins) and whisk the sugar and lemon juice into the strained liquid. Taste. It may need more sugar, depending on the fruit. Transfer to sterile bottles and store in the fridge until ready to use, though it's best used within a month. You can pasteurise this (see page 10) to make it shelf stable and store it in the pantry, too.

1 kg (2 lb 4 oz) blueberries

3 lemons, peeled with a potato peeler, then juiced

about ¼ teaspoon ground nutmeg

1 fresh bay leaf

500 g (1 lb 2 oz) caster (superfine) sugar

# STRAWBERRY & BASIL SYRUP

MAKES ABOUT 1 LITRE (35 FL OZ/4 CUPS) OF SYRUP

500 g (1 lb 2 oz) strawberries

5 basil leaves

2 lemons, scrubbed

300 g (10½ oz) caster (superfine) sugar

**My goodness. How delicious to find a bottle of bright red strawberry syrup in the fridge, just waiting for a waffle to put it on. This one, with its almost aniseedy flavour of basil, is something to savour in the months after the strawberry crop has been harvested.**

*Wash and sterilise enough jars or bottles for 1 litre (35 fl oz/4 cups) of syrup (see page 10).*

Hull the strawberries and cut them in half. Put them in a large heatproof bowl with the basil leaves. Juice the lemons, reserving the juice, and add the lemon halves to the bowl with the strawberries.

Boil 1 litre (35 fl oz/4 cups) of water (make sure it's only just boiled as it needs that heat to do its magic) and tip this water over the fruit. Allow the fruit to steep for 1 hour or until cool. Drain the fruit through a sieve, ideally a conical sieve because of the way it drains, allowing gravity to do the work rather than pressing it through. That way you'll end up with a lovely red syrup that isn't cloudy.

Whisk in the sugar and lemon juice and taste. It should have a concentrated strawberry flavour. Transfer to the sterile jars or bottles and store in the fridge for up to 3 months. It tastes amazing over ice cream (white pepper ice cream even!), is great on pancakes and the like, but can be thinned out to about quarter strength to make a drink.

# SPICED RHUBARB SQUASH *to have with gin (or ricotta ...)*

MAKES ABOUT 1 LITRE (35 FL OZ/4 CUPS)

There's a lot to love about the interplay of rhubarb and spice. Add a touch of gin (for the grown-ups) and you've a pretty nice way to end the day. Don't dilute it, and you can splash the syrup on mascarpone, use it with a light ricotta dessert, or turn it into a pretty heady granita by whisking as it freezes.

*Wash and sterilise enough jars or bottles for 1 litre (35 fl oz/4 cups) of syrup (see page 10).*

Heat 1 litre (35 fl oz/4 cups) of water in a medium saucepan over high heat and add the juniper berries, coriander seeds and mace blades. Bring to the boil, then turn it down to a simmer for 10 minutes. Remove from the heat and allow the spices to steep into the liquid.

Hit the rhubarb stems with the back of a knife to break the texture slightly, then cut them into 2 cm (¾ inch) lengths. Pop the cut rhubarb into a really big heatproof bowl or dish that will fit it, plus the lemons and the spiced water. Juice the lemons and reserve the juice, then add the squeezed lemon halves to the rhubarb. Bring the spiced water back to the boil and pour it over the rhubarb mixture. Leave this mixture to cool, ideally for a few hours, while the flavour comes out of the rhubarb and lemon halves.

Drain and reserve the liquid, but don't push the solids through the colander. Discard the solids. Add the strained lemon juice to the rhubarb liquid and whisk in the sugar. Taste to ensure it's good and adjust sweetness if necessary.

Pour into sterile jars and seal. Store in the fridge for up to a month. This makes an excellent squash with a nip of gin, a splash of soda and some ice. Or use it undiluted as a flavouring for desserts.

10 juniper berries, lightly bruised
½ teaspoon coriander seeds
2 mace blades
500 g (1 lb 2 oz) rhubarb, trimmed and washed
2 lemons, scrubbed
250 g (9 oz/1¼ cups) demerara or other quality raw sugar

# SYRUP FOR LEMON BARLEY WATER

**MAKES 1 LITRE (35 FL OZ/4 CUPS)**

100 g (3½ oz/½ cup) pearl barley, rinsed and drained

40 g (1½ oz) sugar cubes (about 8 cubes; and cubes really do work best: otherwise use the finely grated zest of ½ lemon and normal sugar, but you'll miss out on a lot of the finer flavours without cubes)

3 lemons, well washed and dried

a few nips brandy (optional)

Some things, like barley water, seem like a strange throwback to my Grandad's era. A time of whites for tennis, Horlicks before bedtime and grey roast lamb for every Sunday dinner. Well, some things are worth resurrecting, because lemon barley water is one of those delightful drinks that should never have gone out of style. Here's Fat Pig's version of the recipe. If you don't have sugar cubes, a lesser but still nice result can be had by adding a tiny bit of the lemon zest to the hot barley water, then straining it out before bottling.

*Wash and sterilise enough jars or bottles for 1 litre (35 fl oz/4 cups) of syrup (see page 10).*

Heat the barley with 1 litre (35 fl oz/4 cups) of water in a 2 litre (70 fl oz/8 cup) saucepan over high heat until it comes to the boil. Turn down and simmer for 20 minutes. Strain the barley water through a sieve, reserving the liquid. (Keep the grains to use in soup.)

Rub the sugar cubes over the skin of the lemons, using each side of the cube as a scourer to extract the oils (the clue will be the colour change in the sugar) and popping the cubes into the hot barley water as you go. I tend to find the sugar can dissolve as you rub with some cubes, so when you're ready, you can dip the fruit in the water at the end to rinse off any oil and sugar still on the skin.

Cut the lemons in half and juice them, then add the juice to the barley water as well. Stir well and whisk in the brandy (if using), then pour into sterilised bottles. Allow to cool, then store in the fridge (for up to a month) ready to dilute and make a delicious drink in midsummer. In midwinter you can make a fabulous hot toddy by simply adding a bit of boiling water.

# BLACKCURRANT & LICORICE SQUASH

MAKES 1 LITRE (35 FL OZ/4 CUPS) SYRUP

I make this using fennel seeds, but if you have licorice root, that's even better. If you're not a fan of the aniseed flavour, add 2 fresh bay leaves and 1 teaspoon of allspice berries to the currants as they cook, in place of the fennel.

*Wash and sterilise enough jars or bottles for 1 litre (35 fl oz/4 cups) of syrup (see page 10).*

Rinse the blackcurrants and put them in a medium saucepan with 1 litre (35 fl oz/4 cups) of water, the fennel seeds and lemon peel and bring to the boil over very high heat. Reduce the heat and simmer for 30 minutes, then add the sugar. Whisk to dissolve, then strain the syrup through a sieve, without pressing the pulp, to avoid making it cloudy.

Transfer the liquid to sterile bottles and store in the fridge.

500 g (1 lb 2 oz) blackcurrants

2 teaspoons fennel seeds, lightly toasted

2 strips of lemon peel (removed with a potato peeler)

250 g (9 oz) caster (superfine) sugar

# GOOSEBERRY & SOUR CHERRY SYRUP

**MAKES ABOUT 2 LITRES (70 FL OZ/8 CUPS)**

500 g (1 lb 2 oz) gooseberries

500 g (1 lb 2 oz) kentish or other sour cherries

400 g (14 oz) caster (superfine) sugar

The lusciousness of gooseberry is even better with a little cherry in it, especially the slight almond hint from sour cherries. You can use sweet cherries in this and it's nearly as good. We, however, prefer to use kentish or morello cherries for that extra something.

*Wash and sterilise enough jars or bottles for 2 litres (70 fl oz/8 cups) of syrup (see page 10).*

Pick over the gooseberries and cherries, removing any stalks or bruised fruit. Rinse them well and put them in a large saucepan with enough water to just cover the fruit. Add the sugar and bring to the boil over high heat. Reduce the heat and simmer for 10 minutes, then remove from the heat and press the fruit through a sieve. Discard the seeds and solids and keep any juices or pulp. Taste for sweetness (the sugar should have pretty much dominated the sourness of the gooseberries, but it can vary). Store in sterilised jars in the fridge, and if pasteurised (see page 10), it can keep in the pantry for up to a year. Keep it in the fridge once opened.

Use the syrup on waffles, on crepes, in drinks, over other fruit, in a sundae, or to liven up a trifle with summery flavours in midwinter.

# CHAPTER EIGHT:
## Dried + Candied + Pastes

*Smoked Apple Paste*
recipe page 191

You don't have to dry your own mushrooms. Or make your own fruit pastes. (Just as you don't have to make your own jam or bottle your own sauce.) But if you've the time, the raw ingredients and the desire, these are the recipes for you.

Once you've filled your pantry or fridge, you'll find other dishes lifted. Your hot cross buns will be out of this world with your own candied citrus peel. A ricotta dessert will be given a kick with some diced candied pumpkin. After-dinner chocolates will make way for little sugared quince comfits. And your cheese platter will be envied when you use smoked apple paste in place of the ubiquitous quince version.

# FIVE-SPICED PEAR PASTE

MAKES 1.5 KG (3 LB 5 OZ) OR SO

This paste is a good alternative to quince paste.
It's sweet, yet savoury after a fashion. A small bit goes
a long way. Without the five-spice it's the perfect foil
for blue cheese; with it, it's a more likely pair with
goat's cheese or even a hard cheese that's almost
parmesan in style.

Wash the pears and cut them into large chunks. Put them in
a saucepan and add 1 litre (35 fl oz/4 cups) of water. Bring to
the boil and simmer until soft.

Push the fruit through a mouli (food mill) or sieve. Combine
the purée with the sugar in a jam pan or similar (see page 15),
and stir over medium–high heat until the sugar is dissolved.
Reduce the heat and add the lemon zest and juice and the
five-spice. Continue stirring until really thick, which could
take over an hour or even two, depending on your pan. It's
ready when the spoon leaves a gap when stirred.

Scoop this mixture into an oiled or silicone paper-lined
20 x 30 cm (8 x 12 inch) baking dish. Smooth the top with
an oiled rubber spatula. Allow to cool overnight.

To serve, take the paste out of the dish, and cut it into serving
pieces. Keeps for 3–4 months wrapped in greaseproof paper
in an airtight container.

3 kg (6 lb 12 oz) ripe pears
900 g (2 lb) sugar
zest and juice of 1 lemon
1 teaspoon Chinese five-spice

# SMOKED APPLE PASTE

**MAKES ABOUT 1.5 KG (3 LB 5 OZ) PASTE**

2 kg (4 lb 8 oz) apples, a mixture
of kinds such as cox's orange
pippin, golden delicious and
pink ladies

900 g (2 lb) sugar

generous handful smoking chips

a splash or two of walnut oil

**A subtle smoky hint is given to a classic apple paste to make it more delicious, more unctuous, more snazzy.**

Wash the apples, chop them up, including the peel and cores, and put them in a large saucepan. Add 1 litre (35 fl oz/4 cups) of water and cover. Bring to the boil over high heat, then reduce the heat and simmer until the apple is very soft. Push through a very fine food mill or, if you're strong, push it through a fine sieve. Don't be tempted to purée it in a food processor because the seeds won't make for a nice flavour once mulched. Return the pulp to the stove in a jam pan or clean saucepan over medium heat and add the sugar. When it boils, turn the heat down very low and stir, stir, stir until thick and dark and fudgy. You can only walk away for a small amount of time between stirs. Otherwise, turn it off until you've got time to stand in the kitchen and stir it again. I like to do this kind of thing when I'm in the kitchen anyway. Stir until it's so thick it leaves a stir line to the bottom of the pan when you take out the spatula.

Brush a 20 x 30 cm (8 x 12 inch) baking tin with walnut oil, pour in the paste, flatten evenly and allow to set.

Now comes the smoking part: get a really large metal roasting tin, sprinkle a pile of woodchips in the base and add a wire rack. Remove the apple paste slab from the tin and set it on the rack. Place the roasting tin over a really high heat—a gas flame is best—just where the pile of chips are. When the chips start smoking, quickly seal the entire tin in foil. Smoke for 5 minutes, or when the smoky flavour is to your liking.

# DRIED CITRUS PEEL

**Dried peel is useful for all kinds of dishes, from savoury to sweet. It's often wasted when you eat the fruit or squeeze the juice, when a little drying can yield plenty of extra flavour for months to come.**

Any citrus works well: lemons, oranges, mandarins or grapefruit. Ideally, use organic fruit that's not waxed, to avoid any untoward bits that may be on the skin.

Wash the fruit to remove any dust, or scrub a little to remove any wax on the skin and peel off those pesky bloody stickers. Take thin strips off the fruit with a peeler. Thread the peel onto a piece of sewing cotton using a needle. Hang in a warm place to dry for a few days. Over the oven works well, particularly if you're baking much, or have a wood cooker or heater. Alternatively, place on a baking tray in a warming oven overnight, at around 60°C (140°F). If they feel a bit flabby in the morning give them a few more hours. You'll know they are done when they are quite stiff.

Store in a glass jar or leave to hang in your kitchen and use as required. Most citrus peel is gorgeous in hearty beef stews. Dried mandarin peel can pair expertly with star anise to make some excellent Chinese dishes. And the peel can be pulverised in a spice grinder to make a zesty sprinkle dust to use on cakes and yoghurt or over salads.

# QUINCE COMFITS

**MAKES ABOUT 1.2 KG (2 LB 10 OZ)**

Comfits are little sugar-coated titbits. Because quince paste seems such a commonplace thing these days, we thought we'd give you something else to do with quinces.

4 large quinces, about 1.4 kg (3 lb 2 oz)

700 g (1 lb 9 oz) caster (superfine) sugar, plus extra for coating

*Preheat the oven to 180°C (350°F).*

Place the whole unpeeled quinces on a baking tray, cover with foil and bake until soft. That'll take a bit over an hour or thereabouts. Roughly mash them a bit and push through a mouli or sieve.

Pop the quince pulp and the sugar in a jam pan and put the pan over medium heat. Stir until the sugar has dissolved, then continue to cook over very low heat, stirring often, until the quince is dark ruby red and very stiff. Pour into a lightly oiled 22 cm (8¼ inch) square cake tin, smoothing the top with an oiled spatula, and allow to set overnight. Slice into mouthful-size squares then toss in extra caster sugar. Keeps in an airtight container for several weeks.

# DAMSON CHEESE

**MAKES ABOUT 2.5 KG (5 LB 8 OZ)**

2 kg (4 lb 8 oz) damson plums

about 1 kg (2 lb 4 oz) sugar

**Damson cheese is a very old recipe. It isn't a cheese in the dairy sense but a thick fruity paste; a throwback to when the term 'cheese' was used more loosely. It is mysteriously inky and black and should keep for years.**

*Wash and sterilise five or six 300 ml (10½ fl oz) straight-sided jars (see page 10). Preheat the oven to 150°C (300°F).*

Place the damsons in a cast-iron casserole dish with a well-fitting lid. Bake for about an hour until the juice runs freely and the stones become loose. Push the fruit and juice through a sieve. Collect some of the stones, crack them to remove the kernels and add these to the pulp. This seems like a lot of faffing, but they add a strong almond flavour, although it will still be delicious if you skip this step.

Weigh the pulp and put it in a jam pan (see page 15). Add 75 g (2¾ oz) of sugar for every 100 g (3½ oz) of fruit pulp. Bring to the boil over medium to high heat, stirring often and turning the heat down if it's really raging, for about 40–50 minutes until it's set when tested, (see page 18).

Put the cheese in straight-sided jars: this is so it can be turned out onto a plate when ready to serve. It's best to keep for 6 months before use. When it starts to shrink away from the side of the jar it is ready.

# DRIED MUSHROOMS

MAKES ABOUT 100 G (3½ OZ)

1 kg (2 lb 4 oz) mushrooms, sliced about 4 mm thick

By far the best way to dry mushrooms is in a dehydrator that you buy. But you can do it yourself without one and it's worth the effort because, once dried, mushrooms have an amazing deep, almost primordial character that is very different to the fresh version. We tend to dry some of the wild mushrooms we find (not saffron milk caps, because they never rehydrate), because we know what we're doing, but you can dry normal store-bought mushrooms and get similarly great results.

Lay the mushrooms on paper towel and set them in the sun for an hour or two, turning every 30 minutes or so, to help them start to dehydrate. You can also do this in a cool oven, ideally under 100°C (210°F), and use a wire rack rather than the paper towel.

Once the mushrooms have started to dry, you can lay them on wire racks in a warm—preferably a bit sunny—airy place, and just check them every few hours. What you're trying to do is dehydrate them completely, and not have them stick.

When you think your mushrooms are dry (they'll have shrunk to almost nothing and gone dark and firm), they're not ready. Always dry them for an extra day or two beyond what you think, because if there's any residual moisture, they'll go mouldy in the jar. In fact, I recommend you don't put them in a sealed container, unless you have something to absorb moisture in there (such as a food-grade silica gel packet), until they're really, certainly dry. It's better to use a nearly airtight container.

Once dried, they store well for up to about a year.

# CANDIED CITRUS PEEL

**MAKES ABOUT 500 G (1 LB 2 OZ)**

Citrus peel—most commonly used are orange and lemon, but also tangelo, mandarin, lime and grapefruit—has a lovely aroma from the oils. But the pith, the white part attached to the coloured peel, can make it bitter. Here, we blanch the peel to extract that bitterness, before candying the peel for use in sweets and puddings.

Put the citrus peel into a medium saucepan, cover with cold water and heat over high heat. When it comes to the boil, drain, cover with fresh cold water and repeat. Repeat this process, called blanching, 3 more times (5 times in total).

After the last blanching, put about 300 ml (10⅓ fl oz) of water in a clean saucepan. Add the sugar and bring to the boil. Add the citrus peel and simmer gently for about 1 hour, until the peel is translucent right the way through.

Remove the peel from the saucepan and place on a wire rack or similar so that it drains well. Once cool, store in an airtight container in the fridge.

500 g (1 lb 2 oz) citrus peel, ideally from quartered fruit or similar

250 g (9 oz) sugar

# CANDIED PUMPKIN

**MAKES ABOUT 1 KG (2 LB 4 OZ)**

1 kg (2 lb 4 oz) peeled and trimmed pumpkin (winter squash), such as Queensland blue or butternut

500 g (1 lb 2 oz) sugar

juice of 1 lemon, strained

Candied pumpkin is a fantastic thing to use in fruit breads and the like. It doesn't scare people who don't like candied citrus peel (though I've never quite understood that, either) but it adds a different flavour and texture. In Italy they use zuccata, the equivalent, in various sweets and celebratory breads— particularly those from Sicily—including cassata, though it's also used in panettone. In some places in the Middle East, chunks of candied pumpkin are the dessert. This is our version, which you can adjust for either. A cinnamon stick thrown in while cooking is a nice addition.

*Wash and sterilise three 500 ml (17 fl oz/2 cup) jars (see page 10).*

Cut the pumpkin into chunks, no fatter at any point than about 2 cm (¾ inch). Put the chunks in a bowl, sprinkle well with the sugar and leave to sit overnight, or at least 6 hours.

The next day, the pumpkin should have given up a lot of its liquid so it won't need water. Transfer the pumpkin and all this juice to a saucepan and heat gently, so any remaining crystals of sugar dissolve. Cook the pumpkin, turning the pieces every now and then if they're not covered in liquid, over low heat for about 25 minutes. Cool, cover and leave on the kitchen bench overnight. The next day, heat and turn and cook again for about 10 minutes. The pumpkin is now ready to transfer to a sterile jar or two and can be kept in the fridge.

# INDEX

# ACKNOWLEDGMENTS

While it may be my name on the cover, those of us at Fat Pig Farm believe we are just preservers of what we find around ourselves, really. It's the gardeners, bottlers, canners, passata preparers and jam makers who have gone before, whose traditions we try to uphold.

So, most of all, I'm indebted to the soil of our beloved Huon Valley, and the people who nurture it, especially Jonathan Cooper and Phil O'Donnell who work hoes and plant seeds in Fat Pig Farm's soil.

The lovely photos are the result of a two-decade friendship and collaboration between myself and Alan Benson, who can transform the everyday things we love to preserve and eat into the delectable pages you see here.

Kellie McChesney worked the jam pan with panache and a great attitude, turning words on pages into the spunky jars that now line the pantry.

This book wouldn't be possible without the support, knowledge and outrageous commitment of Michelle Crawford, whose home and kitchen we invaded, whose recipes we plundered, whose knowledge we garnered and whose excitement for the project I found infectious. A big jammy thumbs up for you. I probably owe you a dinner or two. As a guest, not a cook, this time…

I am, as always, delighted that Sue Hines from Murdoch Books has seen worth in yet another food publication from me. To publisher Jane Morrow, yes, see, I did manage to get the manuscript in by Christmas. Luckily, you never did say which Christmas.

For helping find the right tone (and past participles and placing ingredients in the right order), it's thank you again to Barbara McClenahan, Grace Campbell and Melody Lord for the super-duper edit. And enormous respect to Dan Peterson and Jacqui Porter for the lovely design that gives more life and pleasure to the eye than mere words and pictures really should do.

And lastly, thank you to my family. To Sadie and Hedley, who make long hard days seem easy; who make a simple piece of toast with blackcurrant curd feel like a celebration. To my little family who share in the extraordinary life we live on Fat Pig Farm, I owe you more than I can say. Perhaps I can make it up to you in marmalade?

Published in 2016 by Murdoch Books, an imprint of Allen & Unwin

Murdoch Books Australia
83 Alexander Street
Crows Nest NSW 2065
Phone: +61 (0) 2 8425 0100
Fax: +61 (0) 2 9906 2218
murdochbooks.com.au
info@murdochbooks.com.au

Murdoch Books UK
Erico House, 6th Floor
93–99 Upper Richmond Road
Putney, London SW15 2TG
Phone: +44 (0) 20 8785 5995
murdochbooks.co.uk
info@murdochbooks.co.uk

For Corporate Orders & Custom Publishing contact
Noel Hammond, National Business Development Manager, Murdoch Books Australia

Publisher: Jane Morrow
Editorial Manager: Barbara McClenahan
Design Manager: Hugh Ford
Project Editor: Melody Lord
Designers: Dan Peterson and Jacqui Porter, Northwood Green
Photographer: Alan Benson
Recipe Developer and Stylist: Michelle Crawford
Home Economist: Kellie McChesney
Food Editor: Grace Campbell
Production Manager: Alexandra Gonzalez

A cataloguing-in-publication entry is available from the catalogue of the National Library of Australia
at nla.gov.au.

ISBN 978 1 74336 581 6 Australia
ISBN 978 1 74336 609 7 UK

A catalogue record for this book is available from the British Library.

Colour reproduction by Splitting Image Colour Studio Pty Ltd, Clayton, Victoria
Printed by 1010 Printing International Limited, China

IMPORTANT: Those who might be at risk from the effects of salmonella poisoning (the elderly, pregnant women, young children and those suffering from immune deficiency diseases) should consult their doctor with any concerns about eating raw eggs.

OVEN GUIDE: You may find cooking times vary depending on the oven you are using. For fan-forced ovens, as a general rule, set the oven temperature to 20°C (35°F) lower than indicated in the recipe.

MEASURES GUIDE: We have used 20 ml (4 teaspoon) tablespoon measures. If you are using a 15 ml (3 teaspoon) tablespoon, add an extra teaspoon of the ingredient for each tablespoon specified.